How to Pass

NATIONAL 5

Business Management

Peter Hagan

HODDER
GIBSON

AN HACHETTE UK COMPANY

The Publishers would like to thank the following for permission to reproduce copyright material:

Photo credits

p.15 (top) © Gerhard Seybert – Fotolia.com; **p.15** (centre) © Imagestate Media (John Foxx)/Patient Care V3063; **p.15** (bottom) © Monkey Business – Fotolia; **p.27** © AFP/Getty Images; **p.56** (left) © Getty Images/Brand X; **p.56** (centre) © Jeff Morgan 10/Alamy; **p.56** (right) © artstudio_pro - Fotolia.

The text extract on page 6 is from the National 5 Business Management Course Specification © Scottish Qualifications Authority.

Every effort has been made to trace all copyright holders, but if any have been inadvertently overlooked the Publishers will be pleased to make the necessary arrangements at the first opportunity.

Although every effort has been made to ensure that website addresses are correct at time of going to press, Hodder Gibson cannot be held responsible for the content of any website mentioned in this book. It is sometimes possible to find a relocated web page by typing in the address of the home page for a website in the URL window of your browser.

Hachette UK's policy is to use papers that are natural, renewable and recyclable products and made from wood grown in sustainable forests. The logging and manufacturing processes are expected to conform to the environmental regulations of the country of origin.

Orders: please contact Bookpoint Ltd, 130 Park Drive, Abingdon, Oxon OX14 4SE. Telephone: (44) 01235 827720. Fax: (44) 01235 400454. Lines are open 9.00–5.00, Monday to Saturday, with a 24-hour message answering service. Visit our website at www.hoddereducation.co.uk. Hodder Gibson can be contacted direct on: Tel: 0141 848 1609; Fax: 0141 889 6315; email: hoddergibson@hodder.co.uk

Cover photo © alphaspirit - Fotolia.com
Illustrations by Emma Golley at Redmoor Design and Aptara, Inc.
Typeset in 13/15 Cronos Pro by Aptara, Inc.
Printed in Spain
A catalogue record for this title is available from the British Library
ISBN: 978 1 4441 8738 0

Contents

Introduction 1

The course 6

Course content 6

Assessment 8

Unit 1 Understanding business 14

Chapter 1 Objectives and activities of businesses ... 14

Chapter 2 Factors impacting on businesses 25

Unit 2 Management of people and finance 32

Chapter 3 Management of people 32

Chapter 4 Management of finance 36

Unit 3 Management of marketing and operations ... 47

Chapter 5 Management of marketing 47

Chapter 6 Management of operations 54

Exam practice 60

Answers and exam practice solutions 64

Introduction

This book is here to help you get the best possible grade you can from studying Business Management at National 5 level. Hopefully that will be an A, but not everyone can achieve a top level pass. You could use this book to guide you through the internal assessment process as well as to help you prepare for the final exam.

It is not a textbook and doesn't include everything you need to know for the exam in great detail. It should be used alongside the notes or textbook provided by your teacher but also, more importantly, with the notes and exercises you have done as part of your own hard work throughout the course.

So, how do you pass Business Management?

My students often say to me (after they have got their results) that Business Management is 'just common sense really', and that is true, but I'm sure teachers of other subjects would say that their subject is only common sense as well. The difference with Business Management is that the topics we study influence our lives in fairly obvious ways.

For some students you might as well call Physics 'Magic', as they find it hard to connect with what they are being taught. You switch on a light, your phone or your iPod and it works! You don't really need to know anything more. Someone else has done all the hard work.

What you do need and want to do, is to find out which phone you should buy, what contract you should go with, what features it should have. That is what Business Management is all about, not just from your point of view as a consumer, but more importantly from the business' view.

One of the biggest problems Business Management students have is confidence. They worry they might be wrong and they don't want to appear stupid. This often stops them from giving answers that would get marks in an exam. Well, the markers don't know you, they probably don't even know your school or where it is. If you think it might be right, it probably is, so write it down. You have plenty of knowledge about Business Management from your own life and yes, most of it is just common sense!

So, if it's all just common sense, what's the point of this book?

There are two reasons why you should use this book. Firstly, not everyone who sits the exam will pass; someone would be in a lot of trouble if they did. This book is here to try to make sure that you are one of the students that pass. Secondly, this book will try to make sure that you not only pass, but get the highest grade that you can. Would a 'B' be enough? There is only one mark between an 'A' and a 'B', so why not get an 'A'?

Right let's get started. There is you, your teacher and this book. Between us we can make sure that you get the best grade.

You

Let's start with you. I don't know you, and probably will never meet you, so you need to start thinking about yourself. What are your strengths? Do you find revision easy?

Your learning style

I know when I was your age, I would have lost concentration by this stage in the book and would have been looking for something else to do while pretending to read – sad but true. So well done you for getting this far! If I sound a bit like you feel right now, then you'll be happy to know that it's not your fault, it's just what we call your learning style. It's still a problem though, and if you let it, it will make it more difficult for you to pass any exam, not just Business Management.

There are some very good BBC websites including one that can help you find out what your learning style is, and make it easier for you when it comes time for revision:

www.bbc.co.uk/scotland/learning/studyskills.shtml

These sites can help you find the best way to revise and learn, but they also provide good hints and tips on how to manage your time.

You could also use 'My study plan' app from the SQA website: www.sqa.org.uk. The SQA website also includes such useful things as specimen papers and past papers, together with marking instructions. Although National 5 is a new exam and there will not be many exam papers available to you, you can use the Credit Standard Grade past paper questions for Section 1 of your exam and Intermediate 2 Business Management past papers for Section 2, as much of the course content is the same and it is set at the same level. Just be wary of the marking instructions, they do not always give the type of answer that will get you full marks or even any marks, but they will tell you what you should be writing about. Pay careful attention to any notes that appear under each question as they give more detail on how the answers should be written to get marks.

If you are looking for something a bit different for revision, then the App store at Apple provides a 'GCSE Business Studies' app that covers similar content to your exam. Then there is always the Business Studies Online website (www.businessstudiesonline.co.uk) to help you make your revision a bit different. Just remember though, your exam will be a written paper and at the end of the day you will need to be skilled in writing answers within the time you are given. So make good use of the past papers and any revision exercises or homework given by your teacher.

Get organised!

If you've looked at the websites above, you'll know by now that your brain is a bit weird. You have to teach it what you want it to do. Funnily enough, organising your folders and all your other school work in the real world makes your brain do the same thing inside your head, making it much easier to get hold of it when you need it, say in your exam. It doesn't matter which learning style you have, it helps with all of them. If you must, you can mess it all up again after!

Another good idea is to start a dictionary of key words that you have come across during your classes. It is never too late to get started on this. It gives you a quick reference guide if you forget the meanings of some words, helping with homework and revision, and again organises them in your brain at the same time. Doing it electronically makes it easier to find words quickly.

Your teacher

Okay, I've heard it many times:

My teacher's useless!

Now, I've met an awful lot of teachers of Business Management from all across Scotland, and I can tell you I've never met one who was not trying their best for their students.

Are some better than others? Yes, of course they are. They cannot all be the Lionel Messi or Chris Hoy of the teaching world, but your teacher will be giving you, at the very least, what you need to pass the exam. So no matter how good or bad you think your teacher is, if you don't work with them then you are stopping yourself getting the best grade for this subject. Remember the exams are not there to measure how good your teacher is, they are there to measure how good you are at this subject.

When the time comes for you to learn to drive, you won't complain to your instructor that you are doing the same thing over and over again, practising until you get it right if you are good enough at it to pass your driving test. If your teacher seems to be asking you to do the same thing again, it's probably because it's important to help you pass the exam.

Do the work in class, do the homework, and spend some time looking over what you have done in class that day. If there is anything you don't understand, the best place to get answers is your teacher. They'll be more than happy to help you, even if you think they won't.

Whether you use textbooks, handouts, or copied down notes in class doesn't really matter that much. It's what you do with it that counts. Your teacher will be able to give you many real-life examples to help you understand the topics you are covering and I'm sure that you can come up with lots yourself.

I find that many of the examples I use in class come from news websites on my tablet or phone. I know quite a number of teachers will be horrified to hear me say this, but I also let my students use tablets or phones in class for research or just reading articles related to Business Management. The BBC news website under 'business' and under 'technology' gives me at least a couple of stories a week that are strongly related to what we have been studying in Business Management. So don't be afraid of using what you are used to in your revision.

This book

Okay, now it's my turn to deliver! Here's a quick overview of what you will find in this book and how it will help you.

The course

This section of the book outlines the course content and the details of the informal assessments (set by your teacher) and the formal assessments (the exam and the assignment).

The units

There are three units to the course which make up the three units of this book. These are:

1 Understanding business
2 Management of people and finance
3 Management of marketing and operations.

This book goes through each of the three units of the course, looking in detail at what is included in them, and identifying possible problem areas where students may struggle or where they have struggled in the past. At the end of each outcome are some questions for students to have a go at. These are similar to the type of internal assessment your teacher may use to test you as you go through the course but they are also useful for revision. Possible answers are provided at the end of each chapter.

Exam practice

This section contains some exam-style questions for you to try for each of the units of the course. It contains some hints and tips to help you. Possible answers are included in the final section of this book.

The course

Course content

What do SQA say about this course?

Purpose and aims of the course

The purpose of the course is to highlight ways in which organisations operate and the steps they take to achieve their goals. This purpose will be achieved through combining practical and theoretical aspects of business learning through the use of real-life business contexts. The skills, knowledge and understanding gained are embedded in current business practice and theory and reflect the integrated nature of organisations, their functions and their decision-making processes.

A main feature of this course is the development of enterprising skills and employability skills. Learners will be able to understand and make use of business information to interpret and report on overall business performance in a range of contexts. The course therefore includes the study of organisations in the private, public and voluntary sectors.

The course explores the important impact businesses have on everyday life and therefore gives learners experiences which are topical. It develops skills for learning, life and work that will be of instant use in the workplace. It supports personal financial awareness through improving learners' knowledge of financial management in a business context.

Learners will be given the opportunity to be involved in activities which are challenging, motivating and inspiring.

The course aims to enable learners to develop:

- knowledge and understanding of the ways in which society relies on business to satisfy our needs
- an insight into the systems organisations use to ensure customers' needs are met
- enterprising skills and attributes by providing them with opportunities to explore realistic business situations
- financial awareness through a business context
- an insight into how organisations organise their resources for maximum efficiency and improve their overall performance
- an awareness of how external influences impact on organisations.

Scottish Qualifications Authority

What is in the course?

Below is a list of the topics covered in the course and what is included under each topic. You should cover all these topics during your course of study and should expect to be tested on your knowledge of them through the assessments your teacher provides for each unit, or through the assignment you undertake, or in the final exam at the end. There may be topics that you aren't asked about, but you won't know what they are until the end of the course so make sure you know them all.

Hints & tips ⭐

You could use the following list to start on your key word dictionary suggested on page 3.
If you find you are missing notes on any of these topics before you sit the final exam, make sure you tell your teacher so they can provide them for you or tell you where to get them.

Understanding business	
Role of business in society	Production, factors of production and consumption, satisfaction of human wants, sectors of industry (primary/secondary/tertiary), sectors of the economy (private/public/third).
Customer satisfaction	Methods of maximising customer service and their importance.
Types of business organisations	Sole traders, partners, private limited companies, local government organisations, non-profit making organisations, social enterprises. Understanding of how enterprising skills and qualities help these organisations develop.
Objectives	Profit, provision of a service, social responsibility, survival, customer satisfaction, market share, enterprise.
External factors	Political, environmental, social, technological, economic and competitive.
Internal factors	Financial, human resources and current technology.
Stakeholders	Interest in and influence on the organisation of owners, shareholders, employees, banks, customers, suppliers, the local community, pressure groups and the Government.

Management of people and finance	
Recruitment and selection	Stages and methods.
Training	Methods, costs and benefits.
Motivating and retaining	Payment systems, working practices, industrial action.
Legislation	Current applicable equality and health and safety legislation.
Sources of finance	Appropriate to the types of business organisations in 'understanding business'.
Break-even	Types of costs, profit, break-even point.
Cash budgeting	Interpretation, cash flow issues and solutions.
Profit statement	Sales, production costs, Gross Profit, Net Profit.
Technology	Role of technology in managing people and finance.

Management of marketing and operations	
Customers	Market segments, target market.
Market research	Desk and field methods, costs and benefits.
Marketing mix	Product, price, place and promotion.
Product	Product development Product life cycle: introduction, growth, maturity, decline Branding
Price	Factors to be considered when setting price.
Place	Business location and distribution methods.
Promotion	Promotional strategies including advertising, special offers and ethical marketing.
Suppliers	Factors to be considered when choosing a supplier.
Stock management	Issues associated with over-stocking and under-stocking.
Methods of production	Job, batch and flow production.
Quality	Quality control, quality management, employees, raw materials.
Ethical and environmental	Wastage, recycling and packaging.
Technology	Role of technology in managing marketing and operations.

Assessment

There are three ways in which you will be assessed:

1 by your teacher
2 through the exam
3 through the assignment.

Assessment set by your teacher

You have to pass the assessments set by your teacher to get the full course award. This means that no matter how well you do in your exam, if you have not passed all of the assessments then you will not be awarded a grade for the full course.

It may be that your teacher will have tasks in class that will be used for assessment, or you may have set times for assessments as you go through the course. There are different ways for you to be assessed as you work through the course and it will be up to your teacher to decide which will be used. These assessments will be split into various types. They can be:

- written answers to questions
- multiple choice questions
- research and PowerPoint presentations/blogs/class talks
- workbooks.

Whichever method is used you will still have to show the same knowledge and understanding of the topics covered in each unit.

Hints & tips

Remember that although you can discuss the course topics and will probably be given activities to complete in pairs and groups, the actual assessments given by your teacher have to be your own work.

Your teacher will also tell you what you have to do in order to achieve a pass in the assessment as there are no marks awarded. For example, if two answers are right in a multiple choice question then you may only need to get one right to pass.

Multiple choice questions

Having a multiple choice test for your assessment may sound easy, but they can be tricky to get right. They are certainly easy to answer, you just tick boxes, but picking which box or boxes to tick can be difficult.

There will probably be more than one correct answer in the questions and you will be asked to tick all those that are correct. Let's look at an example.

The questions included at the end of each outcome in the units on pages 24, 31, 35, 45–46, 53 and 59 may be similar to some of the assessments your teacher will give you.

Hints & tips

> ### Example
>
> What is the purpose of a person specification?
> **a)** To identify the experience needed for the job. ☐
> **b)** To identify the job title. ☐
> **c)** To identify the personality needed for the job. ☐
> **d)** To identify the tasks involved in the job. ☐
>
> Now all these answers are about recruitment, and a person specification is certainly used in recruitment, so unless you know exactly what a person specification is and what it is used for you could give incorrect answers as well as correct ones.
>
> If you ticked all four boxes you would get two right and two wrong and therefore fail this question. If you ticked one correct answer and one incorrect answer you would not be showing that you fully understand the purpose of a person specification.
>
> If you only picked one correct answer and nothing else then you would pass this question for your knowledge of the recruitment process.
>
> Of course answers A and C are correct because it is about the type of person that the business wants for the job. The other two answers are about the job itself.

So, in multiple choice tests you should expect to have two correct answers. If you are sure of one, but unsure about the second one then just tick the one you are sure of. If you guess at a wrong answer for your second choice you could end up failing that part of the assessment.

Let's look at another example.

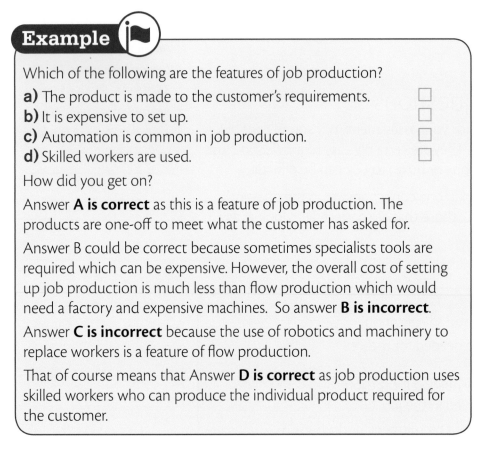

Example 🚩

Which of the following are the features of job production?

a) The product is made to the customer's requirements. ☐

b) It is expensive to set up. ☐

c) Automation is common in job production. ☐

d) Skilled workers are used. ☐

How did you get on?

Answer **A is correct** as this is a feature of job production. The products are one-off to meet what the customer has asked for.

Answer B could be correct because sometimes specialists tools are required which can be expensive. However, the overall cost of setting up job production is much less than flow production which would need a factory and expensive machines. So answer **B is incorrect**.

Answer **C is incorrect** because the use of robotics and machinery to replace workers is a feature of flow production.

That of course means that Answer **D is correct** as job production uses skilled workers who can produce the individual product required for the customer.

The exam

The exam you will sit will come in two parts.

Section one

This part of the exam is worth 30 marks and you will be expected to answer both the questions. The questions will be based around two pieces of what SQA call 'Stimulus Material', which could mean a case study, a graph or a table. The stimulus material is there to help you and to provide prompts to answer questions within the context of the stimulus. The questions can be about anything in the course, so you will have to be prepared to answer anything from your studies. This is similar to the types of questions in the Standard Grade Business Management Credit papers, so you can use these to help you prepare for your exam.

Luckily they should be short answer questions, so don't spend too much time on any one question. Each question will be worth between one and four marks.

The answers you are expected to give will give you an opportunity to show your decision making and evaluation skills, as well as how you apply your knowledge of Business Management.

> **Hints & tips** ⭐
>
> *Check how many marks are allocated to each question to work out how long your answers should be.*

Section two

The second part of the exam paper is worth 40 marks. There will be four questions, each worth ten marks, and you will be expected to answer all of them. The SQA call these 'extended response questions', and these questions will allow you to show your depth of knowledge around a number of topics. The questions will be context based – that is they will be about marketing, human resources, finance and so on. These questions will be more like the questions in Intermediate 2 Business Management past papers but each question will be focussed on one area of the course, whereas the Intermediate 2 questions asked about a range of topics.

The assignment

Those of you who have been counting will already have realised that there are only 70 marks allocated so far. However, the course has a total allocation of 100 marks. The other 30 marks are awarded based on what is called 'The Assignment'.

In class time you will be asked to identify a local, small to medium size business. Your job will be to choose a topic or issue for this business. You should choose from the topics you have studied on your course. For example, you might want to look at a new promotion strategy; raise finance for the business; motivate your workers; improve your customers' satisfaction; or look for new technology you can use in production.

There could be a large number of possibilities depending on the business you have been given, but hopefully the information you are provided with will direct you to one or two good issues you can report upon.

Next you will collect information and evidence from a range of sources, evaluate the information to decide how useful it is and then analyse it by applying the knowledge and understanding you have gained from your course study. Finally, you should provide recommendations for the business to move forward and justify your recommendations.

The assignment is split into two parts – the planning and research stage, and then the write-up of your report. The research can be done individually or as a group, however, each student should keep their own research data they will use in the write-up. During planning and research your teacher will be able to provide you with some assistance.

The write-up will be done under exam conditions in an hour, but will be 'open book' to allow you to refer to your own research data.

An example could be a local business that wants to expand. You could then choose to investigate sources of finance available to the business including: if there is any government assistance; how best to recruit suitable employees and what training would be most suitable; what employment legislation should be considered; what internal and external factors should be considered before deciding to go ahead; what market research should be carried out; and how best to ensure you offer a quality product to your new customers.

Hints & tips

I know that it sounds like quite a lot of work, but don't worry, you will be guided through the process by your teacher so you know what will be expected of you and you will be well prepared for the write-up.

You will already have a lot of information from your course of study which you can use in your research of the business issue. However, there are a lot of very good sources of information for you to get further information for your assignment.

The ACAS website (www.acas.org.uk) will give you good information on employment legislation. The Government website for the Department for Business, Innovation, and Skills (www.gov.uk/government/organisations/department-for-business-innovation-skills) provides information for businesses. Your local council website will give information about population, grants and other types of assistance that are available for businesses in their area. Your local Confederation of British Industry will provide details of local markets and competition. Scottish Enterprise will also provide information on how they can help businesses grow in Scotland, and will provide details of local offices and Local Enterprise Companies that can provide information.

How the assignment is marked

There are five areas of the report that will receive marks.

Background information (5 marks)

The first thing you have to do is decide what your report is going to be about. It should be a small to medium sized local business and a particular issue.

One mark will be given for saying what the issue or topic is, and the name of the business. Other marks will be given for background information on the business or the topic. Each of the points you make should relate to the business that you have chosen.

You could include the following information about the business:
- who owns the business
- when it was set up
- whether it is a sole-trader, partnership, private limited company, and so on
- where it is based
- who its customers are.

Research methods and sources (6 marks)

You must write about what research methods you have chosen and why. They could be field or desk research. You can earn marks by explaining why you have chosen particular research methods. You have to have at least two methods to get full marks for this section.

Marks will be awarded for explaining the choice of research methods and sources. At least two research sources must be used to get all the marks available. Up to a maximum of 4 marks can be awarded for each research source used.

You should not approach the business directly for information, so it may be best to pick a business that has a decent website which provides lots of good information that you can include in your report. A search of newspaper or television websites may add more good information and will increase your number of sources.

If you decide to carry out some field research, for example, a survey, keep the questions simple and straightforward for people to answer. The quicker and easier it is to complete, the more responses you will get. Tick boxes encourage people to respond, but make sure your questions are easy to understand. They don't want to be thinking too much about their answers, so test your survey on other people before you try it for real.

Analysis and interpretation of findings (10 marks)

Here you will look at what your research shows. What you can write here really depends on what issue you have decided on. For example, if you were looking at how the business competes, your research might show that they compete on price, quality of service, location, opening hours and so on. If you mention this in your analysis and interpretation it must have come from your research to get you marks.

Each relevant comment you make should receive a mark, and you can make more than one comment about each piece of evidence in your research.

To achieve the full 10 marks available you will probably need at least three or four pieces of evidence that you can comment on.

Conclusion (4 marks)

Here you will be awarded marks for any suitable conclusions you can make as a result of your research findings.

Your conclusions could be about how well the business is doing, or about something you think the business could do better. You will get 1 mark for each conclusion you can draw from your research.

Collating and reporting (5 marks)

Marks will be awarded here for:
- using appropriate headings to summarise your findings
- making good use of display styles
- consistent use of business terminology.

Obviously using ICT to produce your final report will allow you to present your report more quickly and more attractively. You can produce charts and graphs and include images.

Unit 1 Understanding business

Chapter 1

Objectives and activities of businesses

What you should know 👍

By the end of this first outcome you should be able to:
★ Give an account of the key objectives and activities of small and medium sized business organisations.

There are three parts to outcome 1:
1 Outlining the role of business organisations in society.
2 Outlining why customer satisfaction is crucial to the success of a business organisation.
3 Outlining the objectives of business organisations in different sectors of the economy.

Role of business organisations

It is important to remember what a business is. It is any organisation set up to achieve objectives. Mostly we think of businesses as organisations set up to make profits for their owners, but you also need to know about other types of organisation, why they have been set up and what they aim to achieve.

Sectors of the economy

The economy is split into three sectors.

The private sector is made up of profit-making businesses. This includes individuals working by themselves as well as large companies. Examples include Tesco, a local restaurant, a childminder.

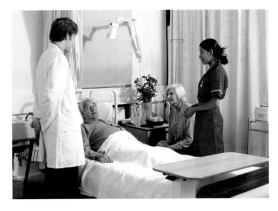

The public sector is made up of organisations and agencies set up by the Government to provide services for individuals and communities. Examples include the NHS, police, fire service, most schools.

The third sector is made up of charities, voluntary groups, clubs and associations. These exist to provide a service that the private and public sector won't do (or wouldn't do well). Examples include Friends of the Earth, Samaritans, a local tennis club.

Types of business organisation

Within these sectors are the six different types of business that you need to know about: sole traders, partners and private limited companies (**the private sector**); government organisations and agencies (**the public sector**); and finally non-profit making organisations and social enterprises (**the third sector**). The table on the next page gives a summary of each.

Type	Ownership	Control	Finance
Sole Trader	One owner	Owner makes all the decisions	• Invest own money • Bank Loan • Borrow from family or friends
Partnership	2–20 owners	Partners make agreed decisions	• Invest own money • Bank Loan
Private Limited Company – Ltd	Shareholders	Board of Directors	• Selling shares • Bank loan • Government grant
Non-profit making	Members or founders	Appointed managers	• Membership fees • Donations • Bank Loan • Government grant
Social Enterprises	Shareholders	Managing Director	• Selling shares • Bank loan • Government grant
Local government	Council	Councillors/ Appointed Managers	• Council Tax • National Government funding • Charges

The sole trader

A sole trader is a person who starts to work for themselves. There are no legal procedures needed to start the business. They can just wake up one morning, and start trading.

This type of organisation is owned and run by one person. The sole trader:
- makes all of their own decisions
- keeps all the profit from the business
- decides when to work
- doesn't have to answer to anyone.

However:
- they find it harder to raise finance
- if they don't work they don't earn any money (for example, if they go on holiday or are sick)
- they can get stressed with no one to help.

The biggest problem is that sole traders have unlimited liability! This means that if the business fails, they are personally responsible for all the business debts. They not only lose their source of income, but they can also lose their home and possessions.

Few businesses are sole traders nowadays. Those that are, are ones that don't need to spend much money to work. For example, a window cleaner would not need to run up any debt to start up or keep his business running as they have few expenses.

Partnerships

A partnership is when two or more people decide to work together. They should draw up a partnership agreement, which is a legal document setting out the terms of their partnership.

Hints & tips

Remember that the 'type' of business organisation refers to the way in which that organisation is set up. It's not about the type of business or goods and services the organisation provides.

A **Partnership Agreement** sets out:

- how much money each person should put into the business
- how much money each person can take out
- how much salary each person will get
- how the profits (or losses) will be split
- what each person's responsibilities are.

A partnership:

- shares responsibilities and workload
- contains the different knowledge and experience from each of the partners
- has cover when one of them is off on holiday or ill
- has more than one person putting money into the business
- finds it easier and cheaper to borrow money from the bank than a sole trader.

However, a partnership:

- has to share the profits
- can fall out ending the partnership
- has unlimited liability.

Partnerships are common among professional occupations such as:

- doctors
- dentists
- vets
- architects
- accountants
- solicitors.

Private limited companies

A private limited company is a business organisation which is owned by shareholders. They usually have 'Ltd' after their name. Shares can only be sold privately and new investors (shareholders) are invited to join the company. A managing director (who may or may not be a shareholder) will run the business.

Hints & tips ★

Remember:

PRIVATE = private individuals (not government)

LIMITED = limited liability

COMPANY = business organisation

It's important to remember that shares of private limited companies cannot be bought or sold on the stock market only public limited companies can do that!

A private limited company:

- has limited liability – so shareholders can only lose the money they have invested in the business and not their personal assets
- finds it easier to raise finance from banks and enjoys a better reputation as a formal business than partnerships or sole traders

- is usually owned by more than one person so the business can benefit from more than one person's skills and experiences.

However:
- the profits have to be split amongst the shareholders
- it can be difficult for a shareholder to sell their shares if they want to
- the business has to submit final accounts to a registrar
- there are legal formalities in setting up the business.

Private limited companies cover a massive range of businesses.

Non-profit making organisations

These are organisations whose main aim is not to make a profit

Charities are run to help groups or individuals in society. To achieve charitable status they must meet one of four criteria:
1 to relieve poverty
2 to advance education
3 to advance religion
4 to carry out activities beneficial to the community.

Charities receive money from donations, shop sales, government grants and fees for their services. They do not have to pay some forms of tax.

Clubs are run for the benefit of their members. They exist to provide a service to people with common interests. Examples would be a golf club or arts and crafts club. They receive money through donations and membership fees.

Both charities and clubs are allowed to take part in some commercial activities to help raise funds.

Social enterprises

A social enterprise is a business that is set up and run specifically for social and/or environmental purposes.

Social enterprises exist to make a profit just like any private sector business. However, profits or surpluses are always reinvested into their social and environmental cause. Their social purpose could be for things such as education, health, sport or community projects.

They can be small or large well-known businesses. Some you may have heard of are:

> **Hints & tips**
>
> All non-profit making organisations are allowed to make and raise money – but they are not doing so to make a profit for the people owning/running them.

The Big Issue

Divine Chocolate

Cornerstone

Edinburgh Bicycle Co-op

Kibble Education and Care Centre

The Homeless World Cup

The Eden Project

There are many different types of social enterprise:
- co-operatives and mutual societies
- social firms
- community interest companies
- development trusts
- credit unions
- housing associations.

What makes businesses successful?

All business organisations produce goods or provide a service or sometimes both! They try to provide these to satisfy people's wants and needs. Everyone buys and consumes goods and services in order to survive, for example, food, but people naturally want more than this – the things people want are unlimited. However, most people can't have everything they want, they have to make choices about what they buy. In order to make a profit and survive, a business has to produce what people want. This creates the cycle of business.

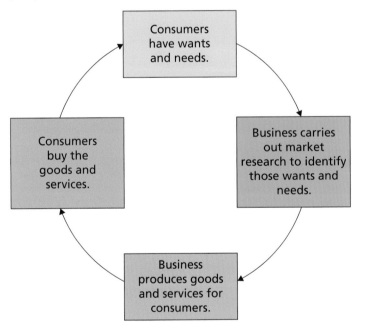

The cycle of business.

Factors of production

In order to provide any good or service an organisation must organise the resources it needs in order to produce these things and be successful. These resources are called the Factors of Production.

They are:
- land
- labour
- capital
- enterprise.

Land

This refers to the natural resources that are used by producers to produce and/or provide their goods and services. They include resources from the land, sea, or air, such as:

- crops
- oil
- fish
- wind power.

Labour

These are human resources – the people that work for the organisation to produce and provide the goods and services. Examples include:

- managers
- production staff
- accountants
- designers.

Capital

These are the man-made resources that are used by the business to produce and/or provide their goods and services. These resources have been manufactured from natural resources. Examples include:

- machinery
- tools
- motor vehicles
- buildings.

Enterprise

This is the skill of creating a good or service. The entrepreneur is the person who develops an idea and turns it into a business:

- They spot a gap in the market.
- They bring together the factors of production.
- They take the risks.

However, business success ultimately lies with the consumer – therefore providing what the customer wants in the way they want is essential for a business to be successful.

Customer satisfaction

Spending time and money looking after your customers brings great benefits to the business. Having a customer care policy, with set procedures is common in most businesses. Happy customers will recommend a business to their friends; will buy from the business again; won't make complaints; won't demand refunds or repairs; will pay higher prices; and will give the business a good reputation. This will lead to higher profits and more success for the business.

We know that customers want the cheapest prices and the best products. However, they also want the process of buying the product to be easy and quick and the business to fix any problems they have

Notes for teachers

Although customer satisfaction and customers have always been in the Standard Grade and the Intermediate 2 courses they are now shown as main headings in the course content. This means that they are a much more significant part of the course, and your students' knowledge of them will have to be greater than it was in the old courses.

without hassle. A bad reputation for poor quality customer service will drive customers away no matter how cheap or good the product is.

So what are the things that upset customers?

1 Talking to employees who don't know about the product

If the employee who is dealing with the customer's question doesn't know the product well, then the customer will then have to go and ask someone else in the business. However, when the employee has excellent knowledge of the product, the customer can get their questions answered quickly, making them much happier customers. Giving all the employees excellent product knowledge will lead to customer satisfaction.

2 Talking to employees who don't seem to care much

Customers usually ask questions because they are interested in, or are having a problem with, the product. When the member of staff makes the customer feel that they are really being listened to, and the employee appears to really want to help, the customer will be happier. So, businesses should train all employees not only to be interested in what the customer is saying, but also to appear interested.

3 Finding it difficult to find the information needed

Being left listening to music on the phone for ages waiting for someone to answer your call, is really frustrating. The way to avoid customer frustration in these cases is to:

- improve the business' website so that customers can easily find what they are looking for
- use call back (call the customer back) in customer care centres when there are long queues waiting for an advisor
- have a good 'Frequently Asked Questions' (FAQ) section on the business' website.
- use tracking systems for the delivery of products so that customers know when they are due and if there are any problems.

Having these options available to customers will reduce the level of frustration they feel when dealing with a business.

4 Having to repeat the problem to a number of different people

Customers can easily get fed up with this kind of problem. There are a number of ways that this can be fixed.

- Giving the person who first takes the call the responsibility of resolving the problem.
- Giving the customer the employee's name and direct contact details rather than having to go through a menu of options on the phone again and again.
- Offering live chat support on the business' website.

If a business gives employees the power to take their time to help resolve the customer's problem, rather than answering the next call within a set period of time, this will make the business appear much more caring. Each individual employee is the face of the business to the customer, so the more they do to help, the better the business appears.

5 Failure to deliver on promises

If the customer is waiting at home for a delivery or a workman and they fail to appear as promised, then the customer will be extremely unhappy. The customer will often have taken time off work, or re-arranged their normal schedule so the business should make sure that the delivery or the workman arrives on time as promised. There is no point promising something to a customer that might not happen, it only makes the business look bad. If a business is unable to deliver on a promise, then their apology should be personal and sincere – perhaps a personal phone call, rather than an email or letter.

If the business follows these points then they will have happy customers. Happy customers will not only come back again to the business, but they will also recommend them to other potential customers who will help the business grow and be successful.

To do all of this, a business will need to:
- develop a customer care strategy which will set out what the customer should expect from the business in terms of the quality of service and how complaints will be handled
- make sure there are enough employees dealing with customer service and these employees are well trained
- have the right infrastructure in terms of the website and call centres
- create a culture of customer service, so that all employees understand the job they have to do
- ensure management clearly communicate the standards of customer services that are required.

It's little wonder that newspapers, television and radio are full of examples of poor customer care as some businesses don't want or can't afford to provide the level of service that keeps customers happy. However, if the business is to be successful in the long run then it has to put the correct customer service structures in place.

Now try this

Try these questions to see how much you now know about customer service. The answers are after them so you can check how well you did.

1 What should a business do to make sure customers will be happy with their purchase?
2 What happens if customers are loyal to a business?
3 What is the purpose of a customer complaints procedure?
4 What is the purpose of a customer care strategy? ⇨

⇨
5   Why is customer satisfaction important to a business?
6   What is an after-sales service?
7   Outline 5 steps that can be taken to ensure customer satisfaction.
8   What are the costs involved in giving good customer service?

Answers

1   ● Carry out market research to find out what the customer expects from the product.
    ● Create a culture of customer service.
    ● Have well trained staff to serve its customers.
    ● Develop a customer care strategy.
    ● Develop a customer complaints procedure.
2   ● They will return to buy from the business.
    ● It will increase sales for the business.
    ● It will help make the business more profitable.
    ● They will recommend the business to other consumers.
3   ● So that all staff know how to respond to a complaint from a customer.
    ● To satisfy customers that if they have a problem it will be dealt with.
    ● To handle complaints in the most effective way for the business and the customer.
4   ● To advise customers about the quality of service to be provided.
    ● To encourage customers to buy your product by giving them peace of mind.
    ● To tell customers what the business promises to do if they have a complaint.

5   ● The business will gain a good reputation amongst consumers for quality.
    ● A good reputation will increase sales for the business.
    ● The profits of the business should increase.
6   ● Where the business provides advice and support to the customer after they have bought the product.
    ● Providing advice and support whilst the customer is buying the product.
7   ● Make sure all employees have good product knowledge.
    ● Train employees to care about customers' needs.
    ● Make the website user friendly, add a FAQ's section, use call back.
    ● Give all employees the power to solve customers' problems.
    ● Deliver on promises and don't make promises that can't be kept.
8   ● Cost of additional staffing to deal with questions and complaints.
    ● Cost of providing web services to help your customer.
    ● Cost of developing a customer care strategy.
    ● Management time ensuring customer focus is maintained.

Objectives of business organisations

Sectors of the economy refer to the private, public and voluntary (or third) sector. Some of the objectives for these different sectors are:
● private sector – to maximise profit, survival, provide customer satisfaction
● public sector – to provide a service, stick to a budget, use taxes wisely
● third sector – to help their cause, increase donations.

Most business organisations share one objective – to survive – no matter what type of organisation it is. The table below summarises some objectives of business organisations.

Objective	Description
Profit	All private businesses need to make a profit. Profits are achieved when the money received from sales is greater than the money spent in the business. Profit is the reward to the owner for starting the business.
Provide a service	Charities provide a service to those in need. Businesses want to provide services for their customers.
Social responsibility	Organisations are part of their communities and want to behave with consideration for their community. For example by: ● avoiding pollution ● treating the local area with respect ● treating employees well ● supporting groups within the community – through sponsorship, for example.
Survival	The business may be the only income of the owner. If the business fails it can no longer provide goods/services the community needs. People may suffer if they no longer get the support of a charity.
Customer satisfaction	Successful businesses have happy customers. They come back again and again. They don't complain. They don't like to buy from anyone else – even if they charge less.
Market share	Market share is the percentage of the total number of customers in the market that the business has. Businesses see having a large market share as a sign of success. If their market share increases it means they are taking customers away from their competitors.
Enterprise	Enterprise means coming up with new products or improvements to existing products. It can mean better ways of producing – lower cost/better quality. This can give businesses an advantage over their competitors.

Questions ?

Objectives and activities of businesses

Write as much as you can for each of the following, then check your answers with the solutions provided on pages 64–65.

1. a) Identify and describe the factors of production.
    b) Identify and describe the 3 sectors of the economy.
    c) Describe what is meant by goods and services.
    d) Describe the stages in the business cycle.
    e) What is meant by the term consumption?
2. a) Describe the benefits to a business of the following:
    ○ customer care strategy
    ○ customer complaints procedure
    ○ after-sales service.
    b) What are the benefits of:
    ○ customer loyalty
    ○ customer satisfaction?
3. a) Describe the meanings of the following business objectives:
    ○ survival
    ○ social responsibility
    ○ profit maximisation
    ○ growth.
    b) Compare the objectives of a Private Limited Company with those of a charity.

Chapter 2
Factors impacting on businesses

What you should know 👍

By the end of this second outcome you should be able to:
★ Apply knowledge and understanding of factors that impact on the activities of small and medium sized business organisations.

There are three parts to outcome 2:
1 Outlining how internal factors impact on business activity.
2 Outlining how external factors impact on business activity.
3 Examining the impact stakeholders have on business activity.

Internal factors

There are many internal factors which impact on a business. You need to learn the ones commented on below. Each of these will restrict what the business can do in order to meet its objectives or meet any of the challenges faced as a result of changes in the external factors.

Finance

The amount of money that a business has available will affect how able it is to meet its objectives. A lack of funds may mean a business:
● is unable to produce more to increase its market share
● may not be able to employ the experienced staff it needs to design and produce the products or to deal with customers
● has to buy cheaper materials which reduces the quality of product on offer to customers.

Human resources

The skill, ability, and number of staff that a business has may restrict what it wants to achieve:

- Skilled workers may be in short supply.
- Managers may not have the ability to make good decisions.
- Owners and managers may be unwilling to take risks.

Technology

If the technology within the business can't do what it wants to, then this will restrict its ability to achieve objectives.

- The technology may not be available to improve production.
- It may be unable to provide the e-commerce it needs to sell online.
- Customers' expectations of technology may not be met.

Technology can also reduce the number and type of employees needed. For example, machines may become computer operated which will reduce the need for staff on the production line but will increase the need for IT support staff.

External factors

There are many external factors that may have a positive or negative impact on the business.

Political

Legal changes

Laws restrict what a business can do. For example, the national minimum wage legislation means businesses cannot pay their workers below a certain amount for each hour that they work. Other laws that can have a direct impact on businesses include:

- employment laws
- competition laws
- health and safety laws
- environmental and pollution laws
- consumer protection laws
- equality laws.

Taxation

Taxes can impact on businesses in two main ways:

1 An increase in some personal taxes (for example, income tax) will mean that consumers will have less money to spend. This will mean that there will be less demand for goods and services. Businesses will have lower sales and lower profits.

2 An increase in business taxes (for example, corporation tax) will mean that businesses make less profit and have less to invest in research and development, new product design and staff.

A decrease in taxes will have the opposite effect.

> **Hints & tips**
>
> Don't get confused between internal and external factors! Internal factors are those the business has control over. External factors are those factors which the business does not have any control over.

Environmental

There are numerous ways in which the environment can positively and negatively impact on businesses.

- Bad weather can spoil crops reducing supply and increasing price. It will also lead to a shortage of animal feed which will push up the price of meat.
- Extreme weather, such as hurricanes or severe snow, can prevent the delivery of goods and reduce the number of customers able to purchase products. For example, heavy snow closed down much of the transport between Glasgow and Edinburgh a couple of years ago. This stopped delivery to factories and shops which in turn led to shortages. This meant business did not have products to sell at around Christmas time, seriously affecting their profits.
- Natural hazards such as earthquakes and volcanoes can have a devastating impact on businesses that are directly caught up in them. For example, premises can be destroyed or severely damaged. However, they also have an impact on businesses elsewhere. For example, the earthquake and subsequent tsunami in Japan forced some car manufacturing in the UK to shut down for the best part of a year as they could not get the supply of parts needed from Japan.
- Temperatures will change consumers' buying habits and increase and decrease demand for certain products. If businesses are not prepared they may miss out. For example, sales of barbeque food and equipment increase when the weather is hot and sunny.

Technology

As well as being an internal factor, technology can also be an external factor that the business has little control over.

- Some places have very poor or no access to broadband internet. The availability of broadband has increased online shopping (e-commerce), making it more important than traditional shops for some businesses. Businesses that cannot access this suffer.
- The increase use and availability of smart phone and tablet computers gives businesses greater advertising and sales opportunities if they can take advantage of them. These new technologies may also mean a business no longer needs separate desktop computers within the premises giving them more room.
- New technologies in manufacturing, are leading to lower priced and better quality products. However, this may involve businesses spending a large amount of money which may not be available. If they don't they will fall behind their competitors and lose business.

Social

As the way society operates changes, the business will have to adapt so they can survive. For example:

- Increases in the number of part-time workers means that businesses have to change their employment policies to suit.
- Consumers are much more aware of green issues, and will look for businesses that produce less packaging, or make their packaging easier to recycle. They will expect the business to be environmentally aware and be looking at ways to reduce their 'carbon footprint'.
- Pressure groups such as 'Greenpeace' and 'Friends of the Earth' can use protests, press releases, publicity, and political influence to change the way the business operates if they are unhappy with their actions.

> ### Hints & tips ⭐
>
> *Remember that businesses won't all be affected in the same way by factors — it will depend on other things such as what the business is dealing in and where it's located. Never generalise in your answers by saying 'all business will…' as this is very rarely true. Use statements like 'most or many businesses will…' instead.*

Economic

Economic factors can have a huge impact on businesses.

Inflation

Inflation is a general rise in the level of prices of the goods and services that we buy as consumers. Prices will go up and down, but if most prices go up and continue to go up then we have inflation.

There are two main causes of inflation:

1. The cost of producing a good or service increases.
2. An increase in demand for a product.

Businesses and government generally prefer a low rate of inflation so costs remain lower for everybody. Large inflation rises can have a big impact as people's wages are effectively worth less so they have less to spend on products and services.

Levels of unemployment

When people are unemployed they have less money to spend on luxuries and are unlikely to plan ahead for future spending on new cars, or houses, or holidays. For many businesses, if unemployment in their area is high that will mean there will be less demand for their products which will lead to lower sales and profits. It may make it easier to find good employees however.

On the other hand when there is low unemployment, businesses will find it harder to recruit new employees and will have to pay higher wages.

Boom or recession

A recession is when a country's economy declines rather than grows. During a recession:

- unemployment increases
- people have less money to spend
- house prices will fall
- consumer confidence will fall.

All this means lower demand for goods and services. Businesses will experience lower sales and profits and will therefore be less likely to invest in new products. They may decide to make some workers redundant, increasing the level of unemployment further.

An economic boom is when a country's economy grows rapidly – the opposite of a recession. In a boom, most businesses start to increase their profits and therefore the number of people they employ and output they produce. They will also be more likely to take risks and invest in the development of new products.

Exchange rates

Many businesses trade internationally – they buy and sell goods with businesses located in other countries. Just like when you go on holiday you have to change your pounds into a foreign currency, so businesses have to change currency when they buy abroad. If they are exporting goods, then the foreign business buying the goods has to pay for the goods in pounds.

Exchange rates vary all the time but if they change dramatically or for a long period of time this can have a big impact on businesses. If the value of the pound falls against other currencies, this will mean that the goods a business buys from abroad are more expensive, which can reduce its profits. On the other hand, if the value of the pound rises against other currencies then the price of UK goods will be more expensive to people buying from overseas and they will buy less.

Competition

Most businesses have to face competition in the market. Their competitors can do a number of things which will have an impact on how well a business does in terms of sales and profit. A competing business could:

- have a new advertising campaign
- bring out new products
- lower their selling price
- introduce special offers
- sponsor worthwhile events
- have better customer service.

All of these things will make a business' competitors seem better, and make consumers more likely to buy from them. Of course the business itself can do any or all of these things to get customers to buy their products rather than their competitor's.

Stakeholders

The stakeholders that you need to know about and the ways in which they can influence the business are shown in the table below. They can be split into internal stakeholders and external stakeholders.

Stakeholder	Internal or External	Influence	Interest
Owners	Internal	Can invest more money or take their money out of the business. Make the decisions for the business.	Owners are looking for a return on their investment – share of profits.
Shareholders	Internal	Can protest against decisions made by the managing director. Can sell their shares which may reduce the share price. Can vote at the AGM, approve dividends and elect the board of directors.	Shareholders want high dividends and want to know how much profit is being retained and why.
Employees	Internal	Can be more or less motivated to work hard. Can take industrial action (go on strike). Can leave.	Employees want good pay and conditions and job security.
Banks	External	Can provide or withhold loans. Can vary interest rates.	Banks want to make sure that the business can repay loans with interest.
Customers	External	Can decide to buy or not buy. Can complain to consumer protection agencies/groups.	Customers want good quality goods at a reasonable/low price and good service.
Suppliers	External	Can decide whether or not to do business with the organisation. Can decide what credit terms or discounts/interest rates to offer.	Suppliers need to make sure that the business can pay for goods bought on credit/ordered.
Local community	External	Can complain to local council. Can organise protests and boycotts.	The local community wants the business to be responsible, provide goods or services needed and provide jobs for local residents.
Pressure groups	External	Can demonstrate, start campaigns. Can complain to government.	Pressure groups want the business to work ethically and to care for the environment.
Government	External	Can vary tax rates. Can introduce new legislation.	The Government wants the business to be legal. It also wants businesses to be successful as that will increase the tax it receives.

Questions ?

Factors impacting on businesses

Write as much as you can for each of the following, then check your answers with the solutions provided on pages 65–66.

1 Describe how the following internal factors can affect a business:
   ○ finance
   ○ staff
   ○ the use of technology.
2 Describe how the following external factors can affect a business:
   ○ environmental
   ○ laws
   ○ the economy
   ○ banks
   ○ the Government
   ○ the local community.
3 Describe how stakeholders can influence a business.

Unit 2 Management of people and finance

Chapter 3

Management of people

What you should know 👍

By the end of this first outcome you should be able to:
★ Apply knowledge and understanding of how the management of people contributes to the success of small and medium sized organisations.

There are four parts to outcome 1:
1 Describing stages of the recruitment process.
2 Describing methods of training and outlining their costs and benefits.
3 Examining methods of motivating staff and outlining their costs and benefits.
4 Outlining current employment legislation.

Recruitment

Once it is established that recruitment for a job is necessary there are five stages in the recruitment process:

1 **Job analysis**

This outlines the main tasks involved in the job. It is used to find out the main skills and experience needed to do the job.

2 **Job description/specification**
   This is a summary of the full details about the job, including the job title and where it is based.

3 **Person specification**
   This is a list of the skills, qualifications and experience needed to do the job. This identifies the type of person needed.

4 **Internal or external recruitment**
   This is when it is decided whether to recruit internally – by promoting or moving someone already employed by the organisation or externally – by advertising the position outside the business.

5 **Advertising**
   This is when the job is advertised and those interested are asked to apply.

Selection methods

There are various selections methods that businesses use when selecting employees for a position.

Application forms give all applicants the same questions and opportunities to describe themselves. This makes it much easier to compare information from a large number of candidates. The application forms will be compared to the person specification to see which appear to match.

Interviews are the most common form of making a final decision on which applicant will be successful. Interviews will be based on who is the best match to the person specification. However, the interview is a two-way process and it provides an opportunity for the applicant to find out more about the job and the organisation as well as the other way round.

Interviews help in the selection process by identifying the personality and characteristics of the applicant. They also give some indication of how candidates react in stressful situations. The problem is that some applicants may be highly experienced in interviews so it is common for other measures such as **testing** to be used. These can be quite expensive and time consuming to run.

- Aptitude/attainment tests measure how good the applicant is at a particular skill such as mathematical skills, typing or shorthand speeds, driving ability and so on.
- Psychometric tests are designed to measure the personality, attitudes and character of the applicant.
- Intelligence tests measure the mental competence of potential employees. They can include tests on problem-solving, literacy and numeracy.
- Personality tests can give an indication as to whether a candidate is a team player or not, and what team role or roles they perform best.
- Medical tests are required for some jobs such as those working off shore, or for some emergency services and the armed forces, where employees need to have a minimum fitness level.

References are used to confirm that the person who is applying for the job is who they say they are. They are normally written statements from previous employers or other reliable people who can give information about the applicant to the potential employer, stating whether they are suitable for the post, how reliable they are, and so on. References should be open and unbiased.

Training

The different types of training you need to know about are shown in the table below, along with the costs and benefits of each.

Type	Costs	Benefits
Induction Training – For new employees.	Need other staff to carry out the induction; will prevent them from starting work immediately.	Become familiar with their surroundings; make them more aware of what is expected of them; settle in quickly.
On-the-job training – While the employee is actually doing the job.	Can make mistakes; will be slow; need to be supervised.	Will be working; won't need to pay for courses.
Off-the-job training – Away from their workstation.	Can be costly; need staff to cover.	Allows the workers to learn in peace without distractions.

Of course, once they are trained, the employees may expect pay rises or promotion which will be a cost to the business or they may leave for better pay elsewhere. Alternatively, there is always the problem that some employees may not want to be trained.

Motivating staff

Staff motivation can be achieved through a variety of methods. These could include:
- training
- staff appraisal
- good pay and conditions
- promotion prospects
- job satisfaction
- permanent contract
- job security
- staff development.

If employees are happy at their work then they are likely to stay with the business. They can plan their future with the business, not only in how they want their job to develop, but also their personal life – when to start a family, being able to get a mortgage, and planning for things like holidays and of course their retirement.

For the business, they don't have to worry as much about staff turnover – having to keep recruiting and selecting new staff. There will also be less staff absences, meaning more productivity. This will give the business a far better chance of achieving their objectives and keeping staff costs down.

Having said that, it doesn't come cheap – good pay and conditions add costs to the business, and looking after staff welfare and carrying out staff appraisals takes up a good deal of management time.

Employment legislation

Employment legislation that you should know includes:

- the Equality Act, which ensures that no employee is discriminated against because of their gender, age, disability, religion or sexual orientation
- the Health and Safety at Work Act, which lists the duties of employers and employees to ensure a safe working environment for everyone interacting with the business, including staff and the general public
- the Employment Acts, which state the conditions and rights employees mush have including maximum working hours, breaks required and the maternity and paternity leave people are entitled to
- the National Minimum Wage, which sets a minimum wage per hour that an employee can be paid.

Questions ?

Management of people

Write as much as you can for each of the following, then check your answers with the solutions provided on pages 66–67.

1 Describe the stages in the recruitment process.
2 a) Identify 2 methods of training.
  b) Outline the advantages and disadvantages of each.
3 a) Describe 2 methods of motivating staff.
  b) Describe the costs and benefits of each.
4 a) Identify and describe 2 pieces of current employment legislation.
  b) Outline how these would affect the business.

Chapter 4

Management of finance

What you should know 👍

By the end of this second outcome you should be able to:
★ Apply knowledge and understanding of how the management of finance contributes to the success of small and medium sized organisations.

There are four parts to outcome 2:

1 Describing sources of finance and outlining their costs and benefits.
2 Interpreting a break-even chart.
3 Interpreting a cash budget to identify cash flow issues and outlining appropriate solutions.
4 Preparing a simple profit and loss statement from data provided.

Sources of finance

There is a wide variety of sources of finance for the different types of business. Not all types are available to all businesses. The table on the next page shows what is available to each.

Hints & tips ⭐

Sources of finance have to be appropriate for the type of business. For example, a private business would not get finance from donations. Equally, a charity could not raise finance by selling shares. However, both types of business could get bank loans. So it is important that any answer on sources of finance is appropriate to the types of business stated.

Source of Finance	Available to	Benefits	Costs
A loan from a bank	All private and public organisations	• Quickly arranged • Can be repaid over a number of years	• Interest will have to paid • Small businesses may find it harder to obtain and may pay higher rates of interest
Commercial mortgage – a large sum of money borrowed from a bank or building society secured on a property	All private and public organisations	• Can be paid back over a long period e.g. 25 years • Can be arranged quickly • Interest rate is often lower than a bank loan	• Interest will have to be paid • Can lose the property if payments are not kept up
Leasing – renting vehicles or equipment	All private and public organisations	• Can get the asset quickly • Don't have to pay out a large sum of money • The asset is replaced when it becomes obsolete	• In the long run it is more expensive than buying • You never own the asset
Selling shares in the business	PLCs and Ltds only	• A large amount of money can be raised. • Don't have to pay the money back • No interest has to be paid	• Dividends have to be paid to shareholders • New shareholders will have a say in how the business is run
Debentures – Long term loan certificates which can be bought and sold on the stock market	PLCs only	• Interest is only paid until the redemption date • Interest payments are fixed • No control of the business is lost	• On the redemption date the full amount of the loan must be repaid • Interest still has to be paid
Hire purchase – where you pay a deposit for the asset you are buying and make monthly payments until it is fully paid for	All private and public organisations	• The full sum does not need to be paid straight away	• The finance company owns the asset until it is fully paid for • It is more expensive in the long run as interest will have to be paid
Grants – money given by the EU or government	All private and some public organisations	• It does not have to be repaid under normal circumstances	• Only given if the business can meet certain criteria e.g. creating jobs in a depressed area
Selling assets – selling something that you no longer need, or selling it to a finance company and leasing it back	All private and public organisations	• The money does not need to be repaid	• If it is leased back, the company will end up paying back more than they received for it
Retained profits – using money from previous year's profits that has not been spent	All private and public organisations	• No money has to be repaid	• The money could be used for something else
Government funding	Publicly funded organisations	• The money does not have to be repaid	• Must stick within the budget set • The money has to be spent as the Government says
Venture Capital	All private organisations	• Venture capitalists are willing to take on more risky investments than banks	• Money is lent to the organisation in exchange for a high fee • They may want part ownership of the business
Owner's savings	All private organisations	• No loss of control	• The owner loses use of his/her personal cash
Donors	Charities	• Does not have to be repaid	• May have to spend money on specific projects

Break-even charts

Break-even is the point where the business makes no profit and no loss. The amount it is spending is exactly the same as the amount of money it is receiving from sales.

This is important because it lets the business know how many products it needs to make and sell in order to become profitable. If it cannot reach the break-even point then there is no point in continuing with the business. The profit is the return to the owners or investors of the business. And they may need a certain return before they are willing to invest.

In order to calculate the break-even point, you have to look at the costs a business has to pay. These are broken into two categories – fixed costs which don't change no matter how much you produce (even if you produce nothing you still have to pay them, for example rent), and variable costs which change with the amount you produce, for example raw materials. When both costs added together are equal to the money received from sales (sales revenue) the break-even point is reached.

Look at the table below.

Units sold	Sales £	Fixes costs £	Variable costs £	Total costs£	Profit/ Loss
0	0	2,000	0	2,000	−2,000
1,000	5,000	2,000	4,000	6,000	−1,000
2,000	10,000	2,000	8,000	10,000	0
3,000	15,000	2,000	12,000	14,000	1,000

From this we can tell a number of things:
- The selling price for each product is £5.
- Selling 1,000 units will make a loss of £1,000.
- The break-even point is 2,000 units sold, or £10,000 worth of sales.
- At 3,000 units the business will make a profit of £1,000.

We can work out the selling price by dividing the sales figure by the number of units sold. So for 1,000 units this would be $\dfrac{£5,000}{1,000} = £5$.

Total costs are calculated by adding the fixed and variable costs together. At 1,000 units that would be £2,000 + £4,000 = £6,000.

We can calculate the profit by subtracting total costs from the sales figure. For 3,000 units that would be £15,000 − £14,000 = £1,000.

The information in the table can also be shown in graph form.

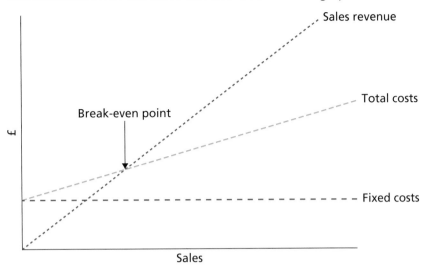

However, we can calculate the break-even point without drawing up a table or a graph using a simple formula:

$$break\text{-}even\ point = \frac{fixed\ costs}{contribution\ per\ unit}.$$

Contribution is calculated by subtracting the variable cost from the sales figure. From the table above, at 3,000 units the sales figure is £15,000 and the variable costs are £12,000, therefore the contribution is 15,000 − £12,000 = £3,000.

The contribution per unit would therefore be $\frac{£3,000}{3,000\ units} = £1$.

It is called the contribution because it firstly contributes to paying off the fixed costs of the business and secondly contributes to the profit of the business.

We can now calculate the break-even point:

$$\frac{fixed\ costs}{contribution\ per\ unit} = \frac{£2,000}{£1} = 2,000\ units.$$

Therefore the business will have to make and sell 2,000 units in order to break-even.

If that seems a bit complicated, let's look at another example.

Example

Imagine you were selling cakes for £10.00 each. The ingredients cost you £3.00, so that would make your contribution £7.00 per cake. If your fixed costs were £350.00, then in order to work out the break-even point all you have to do is divide £350.00 by £7.00. The answer is 50 – so you need to make and sell 50 cakes in order to break-even. If you sell more then you will make a profit, if you sell less then you will make a loss.

Using the same information you could calculate how much profit you would make if you sold 70 cakes. You can do this by multiplying the contribution by the number of extra cakes you make. In this case that would be:

20 extra cakes × £7.00 = £140.00 profits.

Margin of safety

The difference between what you are selling and the break-even point is called the business' margin of safety. So in the example used above, if you are selling 70 cakes and your break-even point is 50 cakes, then the margin of safety is 20 cakes. Your sales would have to fall by more than 20 before you started to make losses.

Cash budgets

Budgets are a way of planning the future of the business. They detail what is expected to happen in the business over a period of time. A budget could be drawn up for a few months at a time, or it could be drawn up for the year.

In planning, the business can identify times when it may run out of cash and therefore address this in advance, or times when it will have surplus cash they can use to buy new equipment.

Look at the example of a cash budget below.

Example

Derek Thomson wants to set up his own sandwich business. In order to get a loan from the bank, he has to give them a copy of the cash budget for the first 3 weeks of the business.

Derek has given you the information below and asked you to prepare a spreadsheet to give to his bank. His opening cash balance for week 1 will amount to £60.

	Week 1	Week 2	Week 3
Opening balance	60	-420	-400
Receipts			
Sales	200	400	1 000
	200	400	1 000
Payments			
Bread etc	40	60	60
Rent	200	0	0
Drawings	150	150	150
Fuel	40	50	60
Insurance	0	70	0
Equipment	200	0	0
Electricity	0	0	80
Wages	50	50	50
	680	380	400
Closing balance	-420	-400	200

⇨

⇨ You can see from this example that by the end of the first week Derek will be overdrawn at the bank by £420, as shown by the closing balance. However, the bank may well give him his overdraft because by the end of week 3 he will have repaid the overdraft and will then have £200 in the bank.

You can see that a cash budget has a fairly simple layout. You start with the cash at the beginning – **Opening balance**; then add any money you expect to come in – **Receipts**; then deduct any money you will have to pay out – **Payments**; and that will give you the cash you have left at the end – **Closing balance**.

Interpretation of cash budgets

What you will be expected to do is examine a cash budget and identify any problems the business may face.

Let's look at another example.

Example

	July	August	September
Opening balance	2000	1090	630
Receipts			
Sales	1700	1200	1500
	1700	1200	1500
Payments			
Purchases	800	850	900
Equipment	1000	0	0
Wages	200	200	200
Telephone	50	50	50
Insurance	80	80	80
Rent	400	400	400
Electricity	80	80	80
	2610	1660	1710
Closing balance	1090	630	420

The most obvious thing with this budget is that the closing balance will be falling each month and if that continues, the business will run out of cash. If they don't have the cash to pay their bills and their employees' wages then they will no longer be able to trade.

Other things that should concern them include the fact their sales will fall from July to September. Although they will pick up from ⇨

⇒
August to September, they are still below the July level. At the same time their purchases will increase each month meaning they will be paying out more for supplies without getting the money back from sales.

They plan to pay out £1,000 in July for equipment which will have a serious effect on the cash position. They could look at waiting until they have more cash available, or they could try paying for it in instalments through a bank loan rather than a one-off payment.

Cash flow issues and solutions

We have seen some issues in the example above and identified some of the things they could do to avoid cash flow problems. However, there are a whole range of issues that could cause businesses cash problems. The correct term is liquidity problems, which means being unable to pay short terms debts.

Common causes of cash flow problems are:
- too much money tied up in stock or buying stock that is not selling as fast as the business would like
- interest rates are too high to allow the business to borrow from the bank
- the owners of the business take too much in drawings
- customers taking (or being allowed) too much time to pay their invoices
- allowing customers to have a high credit limit
- purchasing things such as vehicles, machinery, or premises when you can't afford it
- having high borrowings with high rates of interest
- suppliers not allowing credit or only having a very short credit period
- not selling enough to bring money into the business
- a sudden and unexpected increase in expenses.

Ways of resolving cash flow problems could include:
- offering discounts to customers if they pay quickly
- offering discounts to customers if they pay up front in cash
- selling any unused assets the business doesn't need
- trying to reduce loans by investing more money in the business
- selling some assets such as buildings or machinery and then leasing them back
- asking suppliers for longer to pay
- arranging an overdraft or loan from the bank
- try to cut costs by reducing waste in the business
- advertising to encourage more customers to buy the product/s.

Hints & tips ★

Finance has always been a problem area for students of Business Management in the past so make sure you set aside time to revise it in detail and check anything you are unsure about with your teacher.

Profit and loss statements

Profit is the difference between how much you receive from sales (Sales Revenue) and how much you have spent making the product. Obviously, if the costs are greater than the sales revenue the business will make a loss. Profit and loss statements are produced by the business to show the amount of profit made by the business either as a whole or on one particular activity. At National 5 level, profit and loss statements are fairly simple statements showing:

Sales	The amount of money received from customers in buying the businesses product/s.
The cost of goods sold	How much the business paid for the goods that it has sold to achieve the sales figure.
Gross Profit	The money received from sales minus the cost of those goods sold.
Expenses	Other costs the business has had to pay for such as wages, delivery, telephone, advertising, etc.
Net Profit	The actual profit of the business, calculated by deducting the total of expenses from the Gross Profit.

Below is an example of a profit statement.

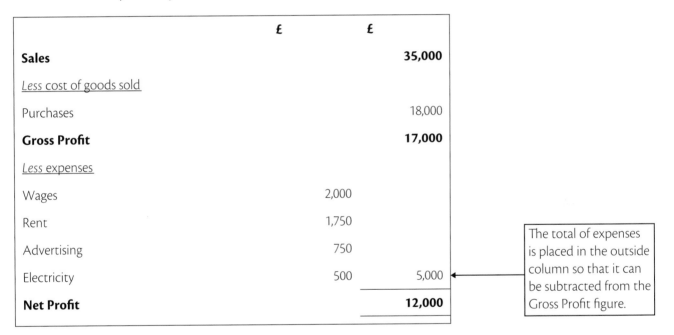

	£	£
Sales		**35,000**
Less cost of goods sold		
Purchases		18,000
Gross Profit		**17,000**
Less expenses		
Wages	2,000	
Rent	1,750	
Advertising	750	
Electricity	500	5,000
Net Profit		**12,000**

The total of expenses is placed in the outside column so that it can be subtracted from the Gross Profit figure.

You could be given a set of figures and then asked to draw up a profit statement using those figures, or you may be asked questions on what each of the terms used, such as Gross Profit, means and why it is important to the business.

Gross Profit is important because it shows how successful the business has been at buying and selling stock. Net Profit is important because it is the overall profit of the business and shows how successful the business has been. It is also the figure that the business will have to pay tax on.

Other items that might be included could be the stock figures at the beginning and the end of the year. You would add the stock at the beginning of the year (opening stock) to your purchases, and then deduct the stock at the end of the year (closing stock). This is because you would have sold the opening stock during the year so that should be included in the cost of sales. The closing stock would have been purchased during the year, but has not been sold. So you would have to deduct that figure from the cost of goods sold.

Another example of a profit and loss statement is shown below.

	£	£
Sales		**150,000**
Less Cost of Sales:		
Opening Stock	2,500	
Add Purchases	65,450	
	67,950	
Less Closing Stock	900	67,050
GROSS PROFIT		**82,950**
Less expenses		
Advertising	8,000	
Rent	15,000	
Wages & Salaries	25,000	48,000
NET PROFIT		**34,950**

The role of technology in finance

Spreadsheets are widely used and you should know what a spreadsheet is and may have used them before in school. Microsoft Excel is the spreadsheet software that is most common in schools, but all spreadsheets do basically the same thing.

The advantages of using spreadsheets are:
- entering numbers in a spreadsheet is faster than writing it out by hand
- there is less chance of errors as formulae can be used to carry out automatic calculations
- if mistakes are found they can be easily changed, without having to re-write the whole thing
- you can use them to easily see the effect changes will have. For example, you could change some figures in a cash budget, to see what will happen at the end of the months to your closing balances. If you decide to change your supplier to one who gives you longer to pay you will be able to see the effect on your cash balances
- figures from the spreadsheet can be merged with Microsoft Word documents to produce things such as statements for customers
- they can be linked to web pages so that customers can see the balance on their accounts.

Of course other types of technology will also be used by finance. For example:
- electronic point of sales systems (scanners at the checkout) can automatically update sales figures

- online banking can allow the business to quickly and easily set up regular payments to suppliers
- online access to other accounts such as the telephone can also allow the finance department to check spending on expenses.

Questions ?

Management of finance

Write as much as you can for each of the following, then check your answers with the solutions provided on page 67–68.

1 a) Describe 2 sources of finance to a business.
   b) Identify an advantage and a disadvantage for each.
2 From the break-even chart below:

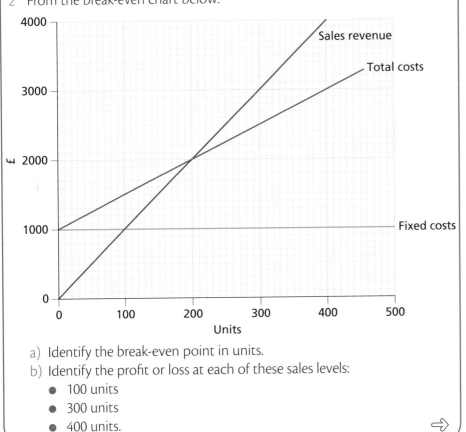

a) Identify the break-even point in units.
b) Identify the profit or loss at each of these sales levels:
   - 100 units
   - 300 units
   - 400 units. ⇨

⇨

3　Define the following terms:
- fixed costs
- variable costs.

4　a)　Identify 3 reasons a business may run into cash flow problems.

　　b)　Describe 3 ways a business may overcome cash flow problems.

　　c)　Use the information below to draw up a cash flow statement:

　　　　Sales £50,000

　　　　Cost of sales £20,000

　　　　Expenses £15,000.

⇨

Unit 3 Management of marketing and operations

Chapter 5
Management of marketing

What you should know 👍

By the end of this first outcome you should be able to:
★ Apply knowledge and understanding of how the marketing function contributes to the success of small and medium sized organisations.

There are four parts to outcome 1:

1 Describe methods of market research and outline their costs and benefits.
2 Outline the stages of a product life cycle.
3 Describe elements of the marketing mix.
4 Outline two ways ICT can contribute to effective marketing.

Market research

There are various methods of market research that businesses use. Primary information collected by field research is information that the business has researched itself. Examples could be postal surveys, online surveys, street surveys. These types of surveys will be looking at what the customer thinks of the product, what price they would be willing to pay for it, how the product could be improved; and also trying to find out what sorts of customers buy the product. This would be useful for things such as bringing out new improved products and knowing who to aim advertising at. It can take some time to collect and is normally expensive to collect and analyse.

Secondary information collected by desk research is information that already exists. Someone else has done the research and you are using it to find out what is going on elsewhere in your market. The information could come from newspapers, the internet (a good place to see what your competitors are up to) or government statistics. This type of research gives a business a good idea of what is happening not only in their market but also in the economy and the general business environment as a whole. It is relatively cheap and is quick to get hold of. However, it rarely gives information directly from customers or potential customers.

Market segments/target markets

It's important to think about how markets can be segmented or broken up. The common ones are:

Age – Different age groups want different products, or different things from the same type of product. For example, younger people want lots of nightlife on their holiday, whereas older people want good restaurants and things to see and do during the day when on holiday.

Gender – For some products, genders have different needs and wants. For example, males and females mostly wear different clothes and use different cosmetics and toiletries. You should be aware that these things may change over time. For example, recent research shows that women now spend more time gaming than men. This is mainly due to the social games on Social Media that can be accessed through smart phones and tablets.

Area – Different parts of the country have their own cultures and their own weather which leads to different wants and needs. For example, Scotland is normally colder than England so there is more need for warm winter clothing.

Household – Young people living alone will have different needs and wants from products than young couples with children. For example, the young person on their own may only need a micorwave and a toaster in their kitchen, whereas the family may need a cooker, washing machine, dishwasher, and so on.

Income – The more money you have available, the more money you can spend on products.

Other common ways markets can be broken up are by education level or by religion. However, people who are in the same groups can still be split into different segments depending on what they like to do. For example, horse riding does not fall easily into any of these groups as people of different gender, age, income and area all enjoy horse riding. This could then be described as what we call a niche market. This is a market that is specialised by the interests of the people that are interested in a particular product.

Product life cycle

The product life cycle is made up of a number of stages, from coming up with the idea for a new product, until it is finally withdrawn from the market. The stages are:

1 Research and development
2 Launch
3 Growth
4 Maturity (sometimes called saturation)
5 Decline.

At each stage the sales and profits for the product change and you will be expected to describe what is happening for each of the stages. The product life cycle graph is shown below.

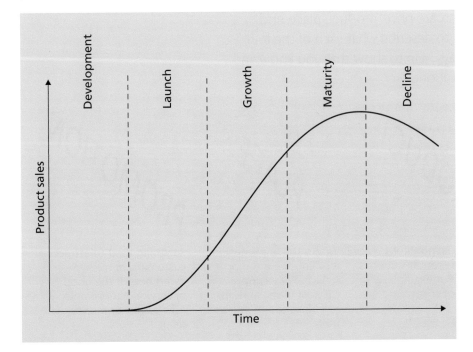

During the research and development stage the business will be spending a lot of money trying to get a product that they can sell for a profit that the customer is willing to buy. This will involve a lot of market research, both desk and field, to find out what consumers want. It may be that the product has to be abandoned at this stage because it cannot be made the way consumers want, or for a price that they are willing to pay. The business will be spending money but receiving no income from the product at this stage. It represents a gamble for the business because they are spending money on a product that might not bring them any profit in the future.

At the launch stage the business will put the product on the market for sale. Customers will initially be unaware of the product, so the business will have to spend a lot of money on advertising to raise awareness and attract customers. Again, a lot of money will be spent with small sales and the product will still not be profitable.

At the growth stage customer awareness is growing and sales are rising. The business will still be promoting the product heavily to continue to increase sales, but later in this stage the business should start to see some profit from the new product.

At the maturity stage consumer awareness of the product will be high so advertising will be less expensive and the profits will be at their highest. At this stage the business should use the profits to invest in the research and development of new products as competitors will bring out products to compete with this one.

When the competition start to bring out better products, possibly at lower prices, and the demand for the product falls, we call this the decline stage. Sales and profits will fall, and eventually the business will take the product off the market.

Marketing mix

The elements of the marketing mix are price, product, place, and promotion. You will be expected to describe what each of the four 'P's mean. Using an example will always help to show that you know and understand what you are writing about.

PRICE	PRODUCT	PLACE	PROMOTION
The amount that an organisation charges a customer for their good or service. For example, '£2.99'.	The actual good or service which the organisation is selling. For example, a packet of crisps.	Where the organisation is selling the good or service. For example, they could sell in shops, or online or a mixture of both.	Anything used to attract customers, or raise awareness of the good or service. For example, a TV advert or money-off deal.

Each part of the marketing mix obviously needs careful consideration and work. For example, there are different pricing strategies that could be used by the organisation. They could use premium pricing which is a high price to show customers that it is a good quality product, or they could use market pricing to charge the same as their competitors, or they could use low prices to try and attract customers.

Ethical marketing

Notes for teachers

Ethical marketing is a huge topic, but in the National 5 course it is included under promotion, so focus on the ethics involved in advertising and other promotional activities.

Business ethics are about behaving in such a way that you do not cause harm to society, or behave in such a way that the majority of people would find unacceptable. Brands that can promote their ethical values are likely to be more successful than those that can't as consumers have greater trust in those businesses.

You probably already know some issues that the Government has or is about to take action on such as a ban on special promotions on alcohol; not advertising certain products to children, and so on.

Truth and honesty when advertising are something businesses must be aware of to ensure that they are not misleading consumers. A well-known example is a big supermarket who ran a special promotion for a product 'Two for £3', when customers could buy one each for £1.20. However, it's not just price, any claims about the product in terms of what it does, by law must be correct. This does not stop some businesses from trying to work round these claims and misleading customers. This would be described as unethical.

You have probably seen adverts on TV from cosmetics companies advertising products to make women look younger. If you listen carefully they don't claim that the product will make women look younger. What they do is tell you that 95 per cent of women who used the product felt that it made them look younger. And that is how the cosmetics company can get their point across while remaining within advertising laws.

Advertising and promotions are often used to entice us to buy things that we know are bad for us but which we want anyway. Alcohol, sweets and fast food are all good examples. But with the amount we consume in the UK the advertisers appear to be winning.

They are also used to get us to buy things we don't really need. How many people buy the latest smart phone even though it is not significantly better than the one they already had which was working perfectly well?

The use of sexual imagery is also common in many adverts. You will be aware of the number of products that use young, attractive people in various states of undress to promote their products. Perfumes and after-shave adverts are common examples.

For advertising to be ethical it must meet these criteria:

- It must not mislead the consumer.
- Whatever it promises must be there in the product – it must 'do what it says on the tin'.
- The advert must not be indecent or obscene.
- It should not offend the consumers' beliefs or moral sense.

Advertising Standards Authority

The body which regulates advertising in the UK is the Advertising Standards Authority. They regulate the advertisements we see in any broadcast or printed media.

The main areas that they concern themselves with include:

Misleading adverts	Rules include having the evidence to prove any claims made in the advert; pricing; the use of the word 'free'; actual availability of products on offer; comparisons with other products.
Harm and offence	Rules ensure that ads do not cause harm or serious or widespread offence. This includes rules relating to loudness of TV ads; shock tactics, unsafe practices and photosensitive epilepsy.
Children	There are rules that must be followed if directing adverts at children or featuring them, such as unsafe practices and unfair pressure, pester power and sales promotions.
Environmental claims	There are rules about making 'green' claims for products or services. Rules cover evidence, the clarity of claims and 'life cycle' of products.
Prohibited categories	Lists products and services that are not permitted to be advertised at all.
Medicines, medical devices, treatments and health	There are a variety of rules on how adverts can use health professionals; rules on evidence (the rules for medicinal claims are very strict); rules on the qualifications needed for those claiming to treat or offer advice; medicines rules; herbal and homeopathic product rules.

There are 32 categories in total, so if you want to see them you could visit their website at www.cap.org.uk/Advertising-Codes.aspx.

Marketing and ICT

ICT is used extensively in marketing. You will be used to seeing marketing on your smart phone, tablet or computer with adverts popping up all over the place to attract you to download or buy products. But businesses will also use the internet to carry out market research such as looking at competitors, carrying out surveys and gathering other information. There are many other uses of ICT as well, both to create actual marketing material and carry out research, including the use of word processing, spreadsheets, databases, and desktop publishing.

Questions ?

Management of marketing

Write as much as you can for each of the following, then check your answers with the solutions provided on pages 68–69.

1 a) Identify 4 stages in the product life cycle.
   b) Describe the 4 stages in the product life cycle that you have identified.
2 a) Describe 2 types of market research.
   b) Identify one cost and one benefit for each type of research.
3 Describe each of the 4 elements in the marketing mix.
4 Describe how ICT can be used in marketing.

Chapter 6
Management of operations

What you should know 👍

By the end of this second outcome you should be able to:
★ Apply knowledge and understanding of how the operations function contributes to the success of small and medium sized organisations.

There are five parts to outcome 2:

1 Describing factors to consider when choosing a suitable supplier.
2 Describing consequences of over- or under-stocking for an organisation.
3 Describing factors to consider when choosing a suitable production method.
4 Outlining methods of ensuring high quality in production practices.
5 Outlining how technology can be used to contribute to effective operational activity.

Choosing suppliers

The things businesses have to think about when choosing a supplier include:
● how long they will take to supply
● the price they are charging (including factors such as any available discounts and whether the price includes delivery)
● the quality of the supplies offered

- whether you want a local or a national supplier
- how much the supplier can supply – how much you can store at a time.

Over- and under-stocking

Notes for teachers

Stock management was covered at Intermediate 2 level Business Management but not in Standard Grade so it's important to note what's needed for National 5.

Consequences of under-stocking include:
- the business has nothing to sell, or may have to stop production
- increased ordering costs
- no bulk buying discounts
- customers buying from elsewhere
- a possible reputation for poor customer service
- increased administration costs due to constantly running out of stock
- loss of sales.

Consequences of over-stocking include:
- capital is tied up in stock when the money could be used for something else
- increased costs for the extra storage – space, equipment, warehouse and stores staff, services, and so on
- risk of stock losses/wastage from things such as theft, accidental damage, stock exceeding its shelf-life, stock obsolescence and so on.

Choosing production methods

There are three methods of production you need to know about – job production, batch production and flow production.

Job production is used for 'one off' products. They are made one at a time. Each job is finished before moving on to the next, and all the products will be different from each other. They can be small or large jobs. For example, both building a new hospital and making a personalised birthday cake would be examples of products made using the job production method.

Batch production is used for making a number of similar products at the same time, then stopping and making a batch of something else. It is often used in the food industry. For example, when making tins of soup, businesses make a batch of tomato soup, then stop to clean the equipment and then make a batch of chicken soup.

Flow production is where products move from one stage in the factory to the next. Each stage is the next step in the manufacturing process. Here you could use the example of car manufacture where each car moves along a production line with a different piece of assembly at each stage, with cars flowing off the production line at the end. This type of production allows for continuous production, with no need to stop.

Which method of production is used depends on a number of different factors. These include the product itself, the finance available, the technology available, and the size of the business. You could not use batch or flow production to build hospitals, however, houses can be built in batches. Setting up a factory for flow production would be very expensive and would only be financially viable for products in mass markets. New businesses are usually small to medium sized organisations, so would not have a big enough market for flow production.

Ethical and environmental

Notes for teachers

This ethical and environmental topic of the course is new and comes under marketing and operations, which is why it's included here. In Standard Grade Business Management, students did consider the social costs and benefits of business, which included some of these issues but it will now need to be considered in more detail.

Wastage

All businesses now consider things like their carbon footprint, the food miles used, their corporate social responsibility, and so on. They will often announce how a change in their operations has reduced the effect of their activities on the environment. A big part of this is wastage – all businesses create waste, just as every household does. Consumers don't want to buy from businesses whose products are polluting their environment as it gives the business a bad reputation which will affect their sales.

The Government has produced a set of laws which govern the ways that a business can operate. So when setting up their operation system they must take account of their legal responsibilities. On the one hand the business will see this as additional costs but on the other they will not want to gain a poor reputation.

By law, businesses have a duty of care to firstly reduce the amount of waste they create and secondly to deal with the waste they do create in an environmentally sensitive way. The laws require them to:
- consider alternatives to just disposing of the waste in landfill, such as recycling
- store all waste produced safely and securely
- keep records of all waste that they transport
- obtain a licence to transport, store, treat, recover or dispose of the waste themselves.

Of course most businesses will use a specialist firm to do this for them, but they have a responsibility to ensure that the firm they use is fully licensed.

Most businesses within the UK will avoid producing products that harm the environment in the UK. However, you should remember that these products may well now be made overseas, especially China, where the environmental laws are much more relaxed. China now has huge environmental problems.

Packaging

Packaging is sometimes referred to as the fifth P in the Marketing Mix – Price, Product, Place, Promotion, and Packaging. There are a number of things that a business must consider when designing the packaging for its product.
1 The packaging should be attractive for the consumer.
2 The packaging should make it easy to carry the product.
3 The packaging should be cost effective to transport.

The Government is also concerned with the packaging that businesses use and has laid down guidelines which businesses must follow when designing their packaging:
- Businesses are required to take steps to reduce the amount of packaging for their products in order to reduce the amount of waste created.

Hints & tips

Remember examples to illustrate your point. For example, the shape of Smarties tubes was changed so more tubes could be put in a box and therefore more tubes could be transported at a time, which reduces their fuel bill and the environmental impact from the fuel exhausts.

- They must consider the amount of materials that they use in their packaging design to ensure that it is the minimum weight and volume needed to keep the product safe and hygienic.
- The packaging must not contain high levels of hazardous substances, which could cause problems for consumers.
- The packaging must be designed so that a certain amount of it can be recycled.
- Packaging that is designed to be disposed of by burning must contain at least 50 per cent paper, wood or cardboard.
- Some packaging is designed for composting, and this must be fully biodegradable.
- Any packaging that is intended to be reused has to be designed so that is can be reused several times, not just once. Once it has been reused it must be suitable for recycling, burning or composting.

Now try this!

Try the questions below to see how much you now know about ethical and environmental issues that should concern organisations. The answers are after them so you can check how well you did.

1 What environmental factors should a business consider before setting up its operations system?
2 What effect would using too much packaging have on a business?
3 What does the Government ask businesses to do when designing their packaging?
4 Why should a business introduce a policy of social responsibility for the environment?

Answers

1 • They should consider the amount of pollution that they may create.
   • Create a culture of customer service.
   • They should consider how much waste their production system will produce and try to minimise it.
   • They should have a policy on how to deal with waste.
   • They should ensure they meet all legal requirements.
2 • It would add additional costs which would reduce profits.
   • It can upset customers who may refuse to buy.
   • They may have to take responsibility for collection and disposal.
   • They may gain a poor reputation for their environmental policies.

3 • They should keep packaging to a minimum.
   • They should only use what is needed to keep the product safe and hygienic.
   • They should ensure that it does not contain hazardous substances in high levels.
   • It should be designed so that much of it can be recycled.
4 • This would assure consumers that they are acting responsibly to the environment.
   • They would gain a better reputation amongst customers.
   • They may find it easier to recruit new employees.
   • They would get better relationships with the local community.
   • Other businesses would be happier to deal with them.

Ensuring high quality

There are various which of ensuring high quality. You must know the details of each.

Quality control	This is where quality is checked at the end of the production and faulty products are either scrapped or reworked.
Quality assurance	This is where quality is checked at every stage of the production process.
Quality circles	This is where groups of workers meet at regular intervals to discuss quality and how to improve it and suggestions are taken to management for approval.
Benchmarking	This means identifying the best performers in an industry and trying to match their quality.
Quality inputs	This means checking that all inputs are off the highest quality. For example: ● ensuring that raw materials are the best that they can be to ensure a quality output ● ensuring that machinery and equipment is up-to-date and fully serviced so that it is working to its best at all times ● ensuring the recruitment process gets the best staff.
Quality standards	This is where a symbol or logo is applied to the product. This indicates that a product/service has met an agreed quality standard.

Technology and operations

For this question you should be able to write about:
● Automated Stock Control
● EPOS – electronic point of sale
● CAD – computer aided design
● CAM – computer aided graphics.

Hints & tips ⭐

Throughout all units you will be expected to use appropriate business terminology and include, where appropriate, the use of real business examples.

Questions ❓

Management of operations

Write as much as you can for each of the following, then check your answers with the solutions provided on pages 69–70.

1 What should a business consider before choosing a supplier?
2 Describe the costs to a business of:
   a) Over-stocking
   b) Under-stocking.
3 Describe methods a business could use to ensure quality in their production.
4 a) Describe 3 types of production.
   b) What should a business consider before deciding on a type of production it should use?
   c) Give an example of when each type would be used.
5 Outline the benefits of using automation in production.

Exam practice

Here we will look at the types of question that you could be asked in the different sections of the exam paper.

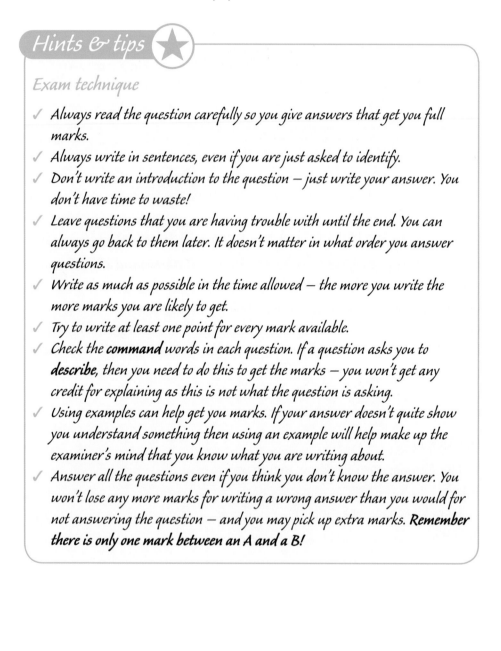

Hints & tips ★

Exam technique

✓ *Always read the question carefully so you give answers that get you full marks.*

✓ *Always write in sentences, even if you are just asked to identify.*

✓ *Don't write an introduction to the question – just write your answer. You don't have time to waste!*

✓ *Leave questions that you are having trouble with until the end. You can always go back to them later. It doesn't matter in what order you answer questions.*

✓ *Write as much as possible in the time allowed – the more you write the more marks you are likely to get.*

✓ *Try to write at least one point for every mark available.*

✓ *Check the **command** words in each question. If a question asks you to **describe**, then you need to do this to get the marks – you won't get any credit for explaining as this is not what the question is asking.*

✓ *Using examples can help get you marks. If your answer doesn't quite show you understand something then using an example will help make up the examiner's mind that you know what you are writing about.*

✓ *Answer all the questions even if you think you don't know the answer. You won't lose any more marks for writing a wrong answer than you would for not answering the question – and you may pick up extra marks. **Remember there is only one mark between an A and a B!***

Section one

Remember in Section One there are two questions each worth 15 marks. You will be expected to complete both. Try the two questions below. There are solutions on pages 70–72 for you to check how well you did once you have finished.

Exam practice

1 Argos is planning to close or relocate at least 75 of the catalogue retailer's stores over the next 5 years. It is part of the company's plans to change Argos into an e-commerce retailer instead of being a predominantly catalogue based retailer. Argos has more than 700 stores in the UK and Republic of Ireland and expects 10 store closures in the current financial year and no openings.

Home Retail Group, which owns Argos, summarised the key challenges facing Argos, including: 'That Argos is biased towards less affluent customer segments'. Following a 6-month review of the Argos business, it has decided to invest in developing a bigger range with universal appeal and a stronger online presence which would appeal to a wider range of market segments.

Source www.bbc.co.uk/news 24 October 2012

a) Other than for selling online, suggest 3 ways in which Argos can use e-commerce technology in marketing. 3

b) Other than job losses through store closures, describe 2 ways the business could cut costs. 4

c) Outline 2 ways in which Argos can ensure that customers are satisfied with the service they receive. 2

d) Describe 3 benefits to Argos of appealing to a wider range of market segments. 3

e) Describe ways 3 stakeholders will be affected by Argos' change of policy. 3

(15)

Exam practice

2   Mackie's Ltd has 11 per cent of the premium ice-cream market in the UK and is the brand leader in Scotland. Mackie's has over 500 cows – the largest Jersey herd in the UK. Jerseys are used to meet Mackie's 'designer milk' requirement because Jerseys produce the creamiest milk.

The process from milking to ice-cream can be completed in under 24 hours. £600,000 has been invested in robotic milking and 9 milking robots have been installed. Since its popularity in the Seoul Olympics, Mackie's of Asia have plans to increase from their current base of 35 branded ice-cream/café parlours to 200 franchises in South Korea. From there they intend to expand throughout Asia, with early plans to investigate Japan. Organic produce is popular in Korea and consumer tests in Korea show similar excitement about a new fresh and natural ice-cream from Scotland.

Adapted from SQA paper 2007

a) (i) Describe the method of production which Mackie's use to manufacture ice-cream.   1

   (ii) State 3 problems of using this method.   3

b) Explain the benefits to the company of having a strong brand.   2

c) Outline 2 reasons why Mackie's has invested in robotic milking equipment for its factory.   2

d) (i) Describe a suitable pricing strategy that Mackie's could use for its ice-cream.   1

   (ii) Justify your choice.   2

e) (i) Identify 2 internal stakeholders of Mackie's.   2

   (ii) Describe the stakeholders' influence on Mackie's.   2

                                                                    (15)

Section two

In this section there are four questions, and again you will be expected to try them all. There will be no stimulus material, just questions for you to answer. Try the five questions below and then check your answers against the solutions on pages 72–76.

Exam practice

1 **Human Resources**
   a) Describe the stages in the recruitment process.   4
   b) (i) Identify 2 payment systems that could be used by an organisation.   2
       (ii) Describe these payment systems.   2
   c) Describe the following types of employment:
       (i) temporary
       (ii) part-time.   2
         (10)

2 **Marketing**
   a) Describe the benefits of selling goods directly to customers.   3
   b) (i) Identify 2 methods of promotion that could be used by an organisation.   2
       (ii) Describe how they would attract customers.   2
   c) Describe 3 factors that should be taken into account when setting price.   3
         (10)

3 **Operations**
   a) Describe factors an organisation might consider when choosing a supplier.   4
   b) Describe quality measures an organisation could use.   4
   c) Identify 2 ethical factors that a business should consider when producing.   2
         (10)

4 **Finance**
   a) Describe the following financial statements:
       • Gross Profit
       • Net Profit.   2
   b) Describe the purpose of drawing up a cash budget.   4
   c) (i) Identify 2 sources of finance available to an organisation when looking to expand.   2
       (ii) Give one advantage for each.   2
         (10)

5 **Understanding Business**
   a) Describe the role of an entrepreneur.   2
   b) Describe 2 types of business organisation in the private sector.   2
   c) Enterprise is a factor of production. Describe the other 3 factors of production.   3
   d) Describe the influences of 3 of its stakeholders on an organisation.   3
         (10)

Answers and exam practice solutions

This section contains possible answers to the questions at the end of each outcome of Units 1, 2 and 3.

Understanding business

Objectives and activities of businesses

These are possible answers to the questions on page 24.

1 a) *This question asks you to identify and describe the factors of production, so you need to name them and then add a description by saying what the terms mean, as shown below.*

- Land is natural resources from the land, sea, and so on.
- Labour is human resources – the people that work for the business.
- Capital is man-made resources such as buildings, machinery, equipment, and money.
- Enterprise is bringing the other factors together to produce a good or a service.

b) *Again here you are asked to identify and describe – so name them and then say what they are.*

The three sectors are:

- The public sector which is set-up and owned by government.
- The private sector which is set-up and owned by private individuals.
- The third sector which is set-up by private individuals but not for profit-making.

c) *This question simply asks you to describe goods and services.*

- Goods are things that you can see and touch.
- Services are things that are done for you.

d) *Here you have to know what is meant by the business cycle. It is often shown in a diagram (see right).*

e) Consumption means using up resources or goods and services.

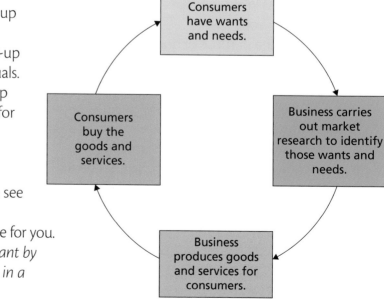

2 a) *Here you will have to describe how having each of these will benefit the business.*
- A customer care strategy will inform customers how complaints will be handled and about the quality of service to be provided.
- A customer complaints procedure will make sure that all staff know how to handle complaints effectively to ensure that the customer is happy with how they are being dealt with.
- The after-sales service will ensure that the employees can provide the right help and support during the sale and after the sale has been made.

   b) *Again you are asked to describe the benefits. You have to write about how businesses are better off because of customer loyalty and satisfaction. Remember it is a describe question so write in sentences.*
- Loyal customers will buy your product before buying any of your competitors' products and will recommend you to other people. You may be able to charge a higher price. (For example, iPhones are usually more expensive than their rivals.)
- If customers are satisfied they are more likely to buy from you again. You will receive fewer complaints and returns and you will gain a good reputation.

3 a)
- Survival – the business wants to continue trading.
- Social responsibility – to acknowledge the organisation as part of the local or national society and to take responsibility for its actions.
- Profit maximisation – to make as much profit as possible.
- Growth – to increase the size of business.

   b) *This is a compare question. Here you have to make a comparison to gain a mark. The first point below compares the main objective of both types of organisation – why they exist. The second compares them in terms of what might be similar about them.*
- The main objective of private limited companies is to make a profit, whereas the main objective of charities is to raise money for good causes.
- An objective of both private limited companies and charities is to survive.

Factors impacting on businesses

These are possible answers to the questions on page 31.

1
- The amount of finance available to a business will affect the decisions it can make.
- The number, skills, and experience of staff will affect how successful the business is at achieving its objectives.
- The use of technology will affect the production of goods and services and will affect how it communicates within the business and with customers.

2
- Severe weather will affect the distribution of goods to customers.
- New employment laws may affect how the business can treat its workers.
- The economy will affect the demand for the business' product.
- Banks can change interest rates which will affect the profits of the business.
- The Government, as well as setting and amending laws, can change tax rates or benefits which will vary the amount of money consumers have to spend.
- The local community can support or protest against the business.

3
- The owners of the business can invest more money or withdraw their investment.
- Shareholders can vote at annual general meetings.
- Employees can work harder, or they can take industrial action if they are unhappy.
- Banks can grant or refuse a loan to the business.
- Customers can buy or not buy the business' product.
- Suppliers can change credit terms; supply or not supply.
- The local community can complain to the local or national government about what the business is doing or plans to do.
- Pressure groups can create negative publicity for the business.
- The Government can change laws or policies which will affect the business.

Management of people and finance

Management of people

These are possible answers to the questions on page 35.

1 *When answering a describe question you would get no marks for simply saying the stages. For example, writing 'job description' on its own would get no marks. You have to also say what it is.*
- The first stage is drafting a job analysis. This is used to find out what sort of work would be involved with the job and the experience and skills needed to do it.
- The second stage would be creating a job description. This is a summary of the job including job title, where it is based, and so on. This would be used to draw up the advertisement for the job.
- The third stage would be creating the person specification. This would identify the type of person needed to do the job, including the skills, experience and qualifications necessary.
- The fourth stage would be to decide whether to recruit internally or externally.

2 *To answer an 'identify' question you simply have to give the name. Here, 'On the job training' would be enough to get one mark. However, it is always good practice to write your answer in sentences.*
  a)
  - On the job training.
  - Off the job training.

b)
- The advantages of on the job training are that the worker is actually doing the job whilst learning so no cover will be needed and the employee usually settles in quickly. The disadvantages are that mistakes will inevitably be made whilst learning the job and someone will need to supervise the training.
- The advantage of off the job training is that it allows the worker to concentrate on learning so they may learn quicker. The disadvantages are that it can be costly to send workers on a training course and cover needs to be provided in their absence.

3 a) Two methods of motivating staff are good pay and conditions and having opportunities for promotion.

b)
- Good pay and conditions will add extra costs for the business and will not motivate all employees.
- Promoting from within the organisation will mean missing out on workers who were perhaps better suited for the job, and not all employees are suitable for promotion.

4 a)
- The Equality Act ensures that no employee is discriminated against because of their gender, age, disability, religion, or sexual orientation.
- The Health and Safety at Work Act lists the duties of employers and employees to ensure a safe working environment for staff and the public.

b)
- The Equality Act means that the organisation has to treat employees fairly and has to ensure their recruitment policies do not discriminate against anyone in the protected characteristics.
- The Health and Safety at Work Act means the employer has to undertake risk assessments of work activities to ensure that they do not place anyone in danger.

Management of people and finance
Management of finance
These are possible answers to the questions on pages 45–46.

1 a)
- A bank loan is a sum of money given by a bank that can be repaid in instalments over a period of time.
- A government grant is a sum of money given to a business that meets set criteria such as providing employment in a deprived area, or for innovation.

b)
- With a bank loan businesses can get a large sum of money relatively quickly, but have to pay interest, which means more is paid back that was borrowed.
- A government grant does not have to be repaid, however, a business only gets a percentage of what it needs.

2 a) 200 units
   b) • 100 units = £500 loss
       • 300 units = £500 profit
       • 400 units = £1000 profit.
3 • Fixed costs do not change with production, you still have to pay
     them even if you produce nothing.
   • Variable costs will change as production changes. The more you
     produce the more you have to pay.
4 a) They may have bought too much stock.

       The owners may be drawing too much money from the business.

       They are allowing customers to long to pay.

   b) They could borrow money from the bank.

       They could ask their suppliers for longer to pay.

       They could sell assets that they no longer need.

   c)

	£
Sales	50,000
Cost of Sales	20,000
Gross Profit	30,000
Expenses	15,000
Net Profit	15,000

Management of marketing and operations

Management of marketing

These are possible answers to the questions on page 53.

1 • Launch – the product is launched on the market.
   • Growth – customers are becoming aware of the product.
   • Maturity – the product reaches its maximum in terms of sales.
   • Decline – sales fall and eventually the product is withdrawn from
     the market.
2 a) Field research – the business goes out and gathers its own
       information from the market.

       Desk research – the business uses existing research carried out by
       someone else.

   b) Field research is expensive and time consuming to gather, however,
       it will be up-to-date and will not be available to competitors.

       Desk research gives a good general idea of what is going on in the
       business environment, but it may not be accurate or specific to a
       particular business/product.

3 The four elements in the marketing mix are:
- Product – the good or service that the business is selling/providing.
- Place – where the business is located or how it distributes the product to customers.
- Price – the amount that customers are charged for the good or service.
- Promotion – how the business informs consumers of the product and persuades them to buy it.

4 ICT can be used to collect customer data and inform customers of the product.

Management of operations

These are possible answers to the questions on page 59.

1 The business should consider:
- the price they are being charged including any discounts and whether delivery is charged as extra
- the quality of the goods/materials the supplier can supply
- how reliable the supplier is with their delivery times
- whether the supplier would be able to deliver quickly for a rush order if necessary
- the stability of the supplier's business (whether it's likely to survive in the long term).

2 a) Over-stocking could lead the loss of stock through deterioration, theft, changes in fashion. It also leads to additional storage costs.

b) Under-stocking could lead to having no products to sell to customers meaning loss of sales and customers and the business gaining a poor reputation.

3 • They could use quality control where goods are checked at the end of production.
- They could use quality management where all aspects of production are improved. This would include materials, staff/staff training, machinery, delivery process, and after-sales.
- They could use quality circles where groups of workers meet to look at ways of improving production.

4 a) Job production is where one product is made at a time.

Batch production is where a group of similar products are made at a time.

Flow production is where products continuously move through a production line.

b) The size of the market and who their customers are.
The amount of finance available to set up production.

c) • Job production would be used where the product has to be made to the exact customer's requirements, for example, a wedding dress.
- Batch production would be used where the business makes a number of different products using the same staff and machinery, for example, food.

- Flow production would be used where there is a very large market and economies of scale can be achieved, for example, car production.

5 Automation means that fewer workers will be required so wage costs will be lower.

Machines will be more efficient in terms of consistent quality and productivity and they can run continuously.

Exam practice solutions

This section contains possible answers to the exam practice questions on pages 61–62.

Section one

1 a) Any three from:
- keep a database of customer's details
- advertise on other websites
- check their prices and offers against competitors' websites
- create apps for tablets and smart phones
- use push notification to keep customers up-to-date.

b) Two out of these three would gain the 4 marks available.

Identify	Describe
They could reduce expenses	by cutting back on electricity, marketing costs and phone calls.
They could reduce employees' wages	by reducing overtime opening hours or changing employees' contracts.
They could reduce purchasing costs	by switcher to cheaper suppliers.

c) Any two from:
- employing polite/cheerful/helpful employees
- taking actions to reduce queuing times in store
- have longer opening hours
- have a customer care strategy
- have a customer complaints policy
- make sure staff answer the phone quickly
- making sure all staff are fully trained
- carry out customer surveys/questionnaires
- place suggestion boxes in branches
- ensure good after sales service.

d) Appealing to a wider range of market segments should benefit Argos through:
- increasing customers and therefore sales and profit
- improving their reputation
- making them more well-known
- all of which should lead to business growth.

e) Any three of the following stakeholders could be used:
- **Suppliers** could: be asked to provide a wider range of goods; be dropped; receive more orders.
- **Customers** will have more choice of products, or higher prices, or fewer stores.
- **Banks** may be asked for more finance, Argos debts may be reduced.
- The **community** may have fewer job opportunities and potentially empty shops.
- **Employees** may lose their jobs.
- **Owners/shareholders** may receive better dividends.

2 a) Here there is one mark available for describing the type of production and then another three marks for problems of using that method.

i) Description: Products made in a continuous flow on production line/in stages.

ii) Problems:
- All products are basically the same.
- Difficult to meet customer's individual requirements.
- Capital intensive production which can be very expensive to set up.

b) Explanation should include at least two of the following. A strong brand:
- creates a good image of the company so will encourage customers to buy
- leads to brand loyalty which means it will be difficult for competitors to take customers away
- means there is less need for advertising so this will reduce costs for the business
- the brand will be associated with quality, allowing the customer to be confident in buying the product
- will allow the business to charge higher prices meaning higher profits.

c) Any two of the following. Automation:
- means faster production
- means higher quality output can be achieved
- can run 24 hours a day
- can do boring and repetitive tasks which workers would not enjoy
- is less expensive than employees
- can be more reliable than employees
- will be more hygienic than employees.

d) Here there is one mark for your description of a pricing strategy, and two marks for your justification. For example:

i) **Description** – Penetration pricing (introductory pricing) means a lower price is charged at the launch of a product. The price will be increased as sales increase.

ii) **Justification** – Lower price should enable/persuade customers to try the product and then the price can be increased when the product's recognised in the market

OR

i) **Description** – Cost-plus pricing means the price is calculated to be slightly above the cost of production.

ii) **Justification** – Allows the firm to cover its costs and still make a profit until the product becomes more successful. This will allow it to compete at a similar or better price than competitors.

OR

i) **Description** – Market Price means a price that is similar to that of the competition.

ii) **Justification** – Allows Mackie's to compete with brand leaders in the market and have the same image of quality. It will also ensure the product is not over-priced for the consumer.

You could also use:

- premium pricing
- destroyer pricing
- low price.

e) Here there are four marks in total: two for the identification and two for their influence.

Identify	Describe
Employees	can work harder or can take industrial action.
Managers	the decisions they make will decide if the business is successful or not.
Owners	can add in or take out investment.

So, for example, you would get one mark for employees and then a second mark for describing their influence.

Section two

1 Human resources

a) Stages in the recruitment process are:
- Job analysis – outlines the main tasks involved in the job.
- Job specification – full details about the job including things such as the job title.
- Person specification – a list of the skills, experience and qualifications needed for the job.
- Internal or external recruitment – whether to promote or move someone already working for you, or whether to advertise the job outside the business.
- Advertise the job – place an advert inviting those interested to apply.

b) Any two from:
(i) Payment systems are:
- Overtime
- Piecework

- Annualised hours
- Commission.

(ii) Overtime:
- is paid when the employee works longer than their contractual hours, usually at a higher rate than the basic rate. This allows the employee to increase their earnings
- is guaranteed in some jobs as part of the contract of employment
- may be essential to ensure the organisation runs efficiently – for example the Police and Scot Rail depend on employees working overtime.

Piecework:
- is where the worker is paid a certain amount (**piece-rate**) for each good unit they produce and in some cases workers won't receive a basic wage
- is commonly used in small-scale manufacturing
- allows for low levels of supervision
- motivates staff to work hard enough to earn a reasonable living. However, workers will not pay attention to the amount of waste they create. Also workers will work hardest when they want the most money (e.g. before their summer holidays), and this may not be when demand for the product is highest.

Annualised hours
- is where employees are paid assuming a basic working week of 37.5 hours and employees receive the same amount each week/month
- may mean having to work longer some weeks/months or less in others depending on demand.

Commission:
- is payment by reward for the amount of a product or service sold to customers
- can be paid on top of a basic salary
- is paid as a percentage of the products sale value.

c) Temporary jobs:
- last for a short period of time
- often have a fixed time period.

Part-time jobs are when the worker works less hours than those with a full-time contract.

2 Marketing

a) Some benefits of selling directly include:
- allowing products to be demonstrated to the customer
- being able to explain the benefits and technical details of products
- potential customers can give feedback on the product
- providing a personal service
- more likely to inspire customer loyalty.

b) Any two methods below for part (i) with description for part (ii).
- **Newspaper advertising:**
  - can use colour and/or text enhancement to emphasise a point
  - can be aimed at a particular market segment to attract a type of customer.
- **TV advertising:**
  - can use a combination of moving and still images, sound, colour etc. to get the point across
  - reaches a very wide audience but can also be targeted at particular markets depending on the programmes where they appear.
- **Product endorsement:**
  - if a famous person wears/uses a particular product that person's admirers and fans are likely to want that product too.
- **Product placement:**
  - this means paying for products to appear in popular TV programmes or films, therefore attracting viewers to buy the product.
- **Product promotions:**
  - may take many forms but most consist of financial incentives to buying. One example is 'buy one get one free'.
- **Bonus packs:**
  - is similar to promotions but rather than reducing the money a product/s costs it gives more of the product for the same money. For example, '50% extra free' – whereby a consumer gets more for the same money.
- Other correct methods of promotion could include: competitions; free samples; direct mail; fundraising; discounts; introductory offers.

c) Some factors that should be considered when setting price are:
- the cost of production
- what price competitors are charging
- what the company policy will allow
- whether the product image is to be of high/low quality
- what your target market will/is able to pay.

3 Operations

a) Any three of the following.
- The quality should be at an acceptable level for the goods being made.
- The supplier must be able to deliver the required quantity.
- The supplier must be able to deliver the goods at the right time – when the organisation needs them – and are the delivery charges acceptable?
- Is the supplier dependable? They must be likely to stay in business and be reliable to meet the future needs of the organisation.

- The price the supplier charges must reflect the quality of goods received and show value for money.
- Does the supplier give attractive and suitable discounts for bulk purchases?
- What length of credit will the supplier give the organisation (for example, 1 month, 3 months)?

b) Any of the following quality measures could be used.

- Quality control – where quality is checked at the end of the production and faulty products are either scrapped or reworked.
- Quality assurance – where quality is checked at every stage of the production process.
- Quality circles – where groups of workers meet at regular intervals to discuss quality and how to improve it and suggestions are taken to management for approval.
- Benchmarking – which means identifying the best performers in an industry and trying to match their quality.
- Quality inputs – means checking that all inputs are off the highest quality. For example:
  - ensuring that raw materials are the best that they can be to ensure a quality output
  - ensuring that machinery and equipment is up-to-date and fully serviced so that it is working at its best at all times
  - ensuring the recruitment process gets the best staff.
- Quality standards – where a symbol or logo that indicates that a product/service has met an agreed quality standard. This gives an organisation a competitive edge.

c) Ethical factors include:

- the amount of pollution caused by production
- the amount of packaging needed and therefore waste created
- whether the suppliers used by a business are producing ethically.

4 Finance

a)
- Gross Profit shows the profit made by the business from buying and selling goods.
- Net Profit shows the profit after all expenses have been deducted.

b) A cash budget:

- predicts the cash inflows and outflows for a period of time
- compares actual cash flows to the predicted figures
- highlights and identifies periods of cash shortages
- highlights and identifies periods of cash surpluses
- allows an organisation to plan for large future purchases
- helps avoid liquidity problems.

c) Any two of the following could be used (i), one advantage of each is suggested (ii).

Bank Loan – this can be paid back in instalments, spreading payments out over a long period of time.

Mortgage – can be paid back in instalments over a period of time thereby spreading payments.

Retained Profit – this does not need to be repaid as the money belongs to the organisation.

Grant – does not need to be repaid thereby saving money.

Leasing – frees up capital to be spent on other things and makes it easier to change equipment when it becomes obsolete.

5 **Understanding Business**

a) An entrepreneur is someone who:
   - develops a business idea
   - brings together the other factors of production
   - is willing to take a risk in order to produce a good or provide a service
   - initially makes all the business decisions
   - raises the start-up finance.

b) Any two of the following types of private business organisation:

   Sole trader – owned and run by one individual.

   Partnership – owned by 2–20 people who will share profits and decision making.

   Private Limited Company – owned by shareholders and run by a managing director.

c) The other three factors of production are:
   - land – all natural resources
   - labour – the workforce of an organisation
   - capital – all man-made resources such as tools or the money invested in the organisation.

d) Any three of the following stakeholders and influences could be used.
   - Employees – can work harder or can take industrial action.
   - Managers – the decisions they make will decide if the business is successful or not.
   - Owners/shareholders – can add or take out investment or can vote at the AGM.
   - Suppliers – can decide to supply or not; can alter credit terms for the business.
   - Banks – can decide to lend or not, can change interest rates on loans.
   - Government – can alter or bring in new laws which the business will have to adhere to.
   - Customers – can decide to buy or not buy the product.
   - Local community – can complain or protest if they don't like what the business is doing.
   - Pressure groups – can campaign to force the organisation to change.